NATURE OF COLOR

Your Field Guide for Exploring
Color in the Natural World

Kimberly Collins Jermain

Published by Familius LLC, www.familius.com
PO Box 1249, Reedley, CA 93654

Familius books are available at special discounts for bulk purchases, whether for sales promotions or for family or corporate use. For more information, contact Familius Sales at orders@familius.com.

Special Thanks for use of their artwork to:
Felise Simon
Melissa Cox
Charles Shurcliff
Colin Jermain
Mike Dyer
Nadia Huggins
Carsten Grupstra
Kathy Tarantola

Library of Congress Control Number: 2025934341

Print ISBN 9798893960655
Ebook ISBN 9798893960761

Printed in China

Edited by Mikaela Sircable and Peg Sandkam
Cover and book design by Brooke Jorden

10 9 8 7 6 5 4 3 2 1

First Edition

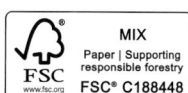

It's a magical world, Hobbes, ol' buddy. Let's go exploring!

—Calvin, *Calvin and Hobbes*

In memory of my older brother, Christopher Robert Collins, who led the way down to the beach, into the water, and out to sea. I am forever grateful for your guidance and your big heart for all living things.

CONTENTS

AUTHOR'S NOTE

Nature inspires my interest in the study of color. Living on the coast, I have always been moved by the sky's changing hue when a frontal system shadows the marsh or the beach at low tide. A dark mass of clouds moving west will appear to compress the sunlit leading edge of the afternoon it is overtaking. What was clear blue, water-like in full sun, is now tangerine.

As a painter, I work as fast as I can to lay down paint in patches of warm and then cool colors, land and sky appearing in three-dimension on the paper before me. The magic is unconscious—the trial and error of scrambling to meet what I am seeing. If I am too self-conscious, I will miss what is unfolding before my eyes that makes this moment of color wholly unique.

In order to achieve an image that radiates the experience of natural color, there is no better method than to work on-site. However, while a season of weather may seem to drone on with slight variation to the casual observer, a landscape painter grapples with visual details that change from one day to the next. Foliage, cloud cover, the angle of light, even the profile of a beach can shift in a week's time, making the practice of *plein-air* painting similar to aiming at a moving target. When professional artists play this game of visual jousting, they use ever more sophisticated tools to reach the prize of accurate color. These tools come in the form of principles derived from different fields of science, as well as concepts passed along via other practicing artists.

Over many years of working outdoors and studying the physics of weather, light, and vision, I have learned that there is both art and science involved in creating an illusion. One day's work painting on location may be one of blissful inspiration and reverie. Another may be a deliberate scientific endeavor to visually capture the mechanics of a temperature inversion on canvas. My goal in creating this field guide is to help you integrate both approaches. This way you can experience more spontaneous success in reading color in the landscape and applying it to full effect in your work and life.

Full Color

There is a lineage of optical foundations beginning for me with nineteenth century artists. Paul Cézanne, for instance, led me to the perceptual principles that illuminate volume and serve as a structural code for making color choices at the speed of light. These fundamentals have been passed down from painter to painter, as I in turn share lessons from my practice with students.

Through the nineteenth and twentieth centuries, painters did not see themselves as objective observers of nature; their work constructing visual images, however, and the way they wrote about their processes comes close to science. Jonah Lehrer makes this point with his book *Proust was a Neuroscientist*, in which he shares current discoveries revealed through MRI technology that were foretold by artists like Cézanne, who was ahead of his time in perceiving the working model for visual perception.

It was an artist who summered near my home on Massachusetts' Cape Ann, Emile Gruppé, who most succinctly defined the nineteenth century theory of color perspective for my use out-of-doors. Gruppé's long career started in New York as a member of a small group of painters known as the Ashcan School, but it was his work outside in nature, often while braving the elements to catch a fleeting subject, that grounded his color skills. Gruppé noticed that making fast color choices enhanced his success because his brain did not have time to confuse, adjust, or distort. In his book *Gruppé on Color: Using Expressive Color to Paint Nature*, Gruppé presents working tips for artists, such as **color perspective**—the use of color to create three-dimensional illusions of depth, especially for creating landscapes or seascapes illuminated by a particular light in the environment.

With my trained eyesight from years painting landscapes, I, too, enjoy trusting my quick response to the stimulus of light. I believe that this confidence in first impressions of color makes it much easier for me to harness and replicate natural light. While it may seem that a quick response in the moment—color instinct—would take years to foster, it is simply a matter of learning optical tricks-of-the-trade.

I have taught color theory for many years, first to artists, then to student designers and architects. When reviewing available texts for my studio classes, I am often at a loss for resources to recommend to those eager to apply color with confidence. The recurring theme is each publication begins the study of color with an explanation of human sight, then uses the construct of a color wheel to make a memorable order to the spectrum of light. I personally never accepted studying the three-dimensional experience of light with a two-dimensional diagram. In researching Josef Albers's personal notes at the Josef and Anni Albers Foundation Library in Connecticut, I found that he, too, rejected the color wheel device.

Albers was inspired by his earlier training and teaching at the Bauhaus School in Germany, which emphasized the relationship between art and science and championed the importance of discovery. His approach advocates for the artist's method of examining color illusions like a laboratory scientist. His breakthrough book in 1963, *Interaction of Color*, focuses on learning the dynamics of color's ever-changing face through experimentation with Color-aid paper. Though *Interaction of Color* ignores volume and color's significance to conceptualizing space (Albers was a printmaker, not a painter), it beautifully illustrates two of the most important theories for working with color: that hue is not static, and that it changes with context and light.

Indispensable Sunlight

Color is essentially light's reflective energy, capable of illuminating the built environment for dazzling effects. Even today, however, color is for the most part an afterthought. In my work with architects and designers creating color plans for commercial and residential projects, the prevailing design process applies color at the end as a decorative element. Rather than defining planes of light with color that can shape the experience of the building's form to craft interior space from the beginning, a white model is typically turned over to the client or a designer to be colored in. Seldom do architectural plans take full advantage of natural light conditions, such as using color for heating and cooling to enhance the interior atmosphere for comfort and use.

Interior design practitioners are still creating color schedules for their projects while ignoring site orientation and relying on information from two-dimensional drawings. Companies that manufacture and sell building supplies use website visualization programs to sell color choices of their products, disregarding site-specific conditions, landscape, navigational principles, and the inherent in-accuracy of photographic technology to represent color. How can this be if color illusion and its powerful visual effects have been experienced through experimentation and practice in the studio by so many for so many years?

Painting from nature, teaching in a classroom, and collaborating with architects, designers, and homeowners on building sites near and far has convinced me that connection to the environment and experimentation outdoors is the key to learning how to use color's advantages. If you take time to immerse yourself in your own natural habitat and explore the simple principles that give color power over our visual response to the world around us, your own joyful color mastery will soon be within reach.

—Kimberly Collins Jermain, Beverly Farms, MA

PREFACE

One day a teacher at my children's middle school asked if she could speak to me about my son Nate. I stiffened with concern. What had he managed to do that needed an immediate conversation? But "What do you do that gets your kids to do what they do?" was the question that spilled out there in the hallway. "Nate takes what he finds outside and makes these amazing things!" She was referring to the small birch log displaying the freshwater fishing flies Nate brought to the Father's Day bake sale. He'd told me that morning as he gathered his things for school that he thought fathers needed something more than cupcakes for a treat.

I responded as I always did: "I open up the back door after school and let them outside."

Exquisite nature has been at the center of everything of value to me from a very early age. It has always been the place where I go when I need to restore my perspective or simply take a break. Given this relationship, I had no trouble trusting nature to guide my most precious children, inspiring them to follow their interests and use their own gifts to respond to the ecosystems of which they are a part, as well as the larger cosmos. Ultimately, this wandering, especially by the shore and in the woods surrounding our home, led each of them to a lifelong respect for nature and for the privilege to behold the world undistracted.

Like most parents, I learn more from my children than I seem to impress upon them. I have also found more to enlighten my life from interactions with students than I ever expected. My gratitude for this exchange bolsters our family's open-door policy to the backyard and reassures me as a teacher that performing simple exploratory exercises outdoors is the best way to guide those in search of useful color skills.

In the beginning of my teaching career, my painting classes were more like science labs. I wanted to explore studio methods informed by chemistry and OSHA regulations, material choices that assisted somatic movement, and habits to make outdoor painting more efficient. I shared color theory from years searching through libraries for strategies that I wished had been passed along to me. I collected articles about perception and tried the experiments out myself to determine if the theories worked as reported. Newly discovered specimens of plant life, weather phenomena, and unexpected colors experienced in my own work (such as the fact that the sky turns pink and individual clouds red when it is snowing at night) provided endless questions, always useful to prompt class discussions.

However, had our class "Landscape Painting" simply made do with photos in the studio to learn how to create realistic imagery, rather than taking on the challenges of working outside, I believe color perspective would have passed us by. I am confident that we would have learned other things, but I am thankful to those who met the challenge with me to be completely immersed in nature. They showed the way to share color's important principles beyond the studio.

As my students and I struggled together to get used to working outside in any weather, we all eventually saw that once the class group made it a habit to engage with nature, our individual fascinations guided all experimentation. There we were, me and my students, all seeking, wondering, making things that sometimes worked out and sometimes did not. What I brought to the outdoor classroom to teach was not what made any difference. Rather, it was the risk of insect bites, the surety of disappointing results, and the persistent charm of nature that summoned the confidence to pursue our uncharted treks. Even though our first efforts to record color's complexity on location seemed like battles at times, it was not having a map that urged us ahead. Also, struggling together made us sympathetic to one another and, in the end, better able to persevere as individuals.

Nature of Color is a simple introduction to nature as an endless resource of joy and ideas. Whatever you do with your field study notes or with the practice of concepts, such as Found Color, I believe you will sustain over time the resilience that comes when you've braved the outdoors. There's something to be gained from every excursion, even when a sudden downpour forces you to gather up your things and retreat from a badly timed outing, or when you've lost your favorite sunhat in the microburst, or when you show up to paint on an island without yellow ochre and nowhere to get it. Nature will train you to prepare, make do, and, of course, be grateful for the opportunity to be outdoors where perceptual gifts reward persistence.

Prompted by the discoveries of *plein-air* artists, I use color to construct planes of light that create the illusion of a three-dimensional landscape on a two-dimensional ground. This cognitive exercise draws also from what I've learned about earth science, physics, and human physiological responses to color in space. Putting it all together, I have trained my imagination to work in reverse. For example, as a color designer on a building site, with paint and building material samples in hand, I can easily intuit the visual outcome for transforming the space with color before it is physically there. My painter's meter-like response to the experience of light has become my mind's eye for problem solving well beyond the canvas. Repeated experiments, and the opportunity to see the outcome of my color choices in both paint and architecture, have calibrated my imagination for predictable performance.

That is my personal experience with color. However, one does not need to embark on a career as a landscape painter or architectural color designer to gain these skills and apply color thoughtfully to everyday uses. To advocate for a particular color, in any setting, you will be better equipped when you understand the strategies of spatial color, passed down from pioneering artists and scientists. You then can be inventive with *color perspective* gleaned in large part from hikes, beach walks, and other outside activities where you are immersed in the natural world.

Nature of Color is designed as a field guide for people of all ages and levels of interest. Passionate hikers and nature lovers already know to feed their innate curiosity with each trip into the wild. Those who might need encouragement to explore nature regularly—and deeply look at what they find there—can use *Nature of Color* simply for fun ideas with family and friends. There is no one preferred way to make nature meaningful. Getting outside is just the beginning of exploring and expanding your color vision.

Bring *Nature of Color* with you whenever you venture outside. As a place for recording color ideas, this workbook is yours to play with, to store a log of unknown plants and animals, to house pressed leaves and flowers, to construct a palette recorded with paint chips, or to recreate a curious sighting with a color painting tool. If you like to draw your ideas, you might want more paper. If you've never tried to draw and are uncomfortable with the look of your handmade marks, use this field guide to hold loose paper, tucked in for safe keeping, to hold your first artful attempts.

I have written *Nature of Color* with friends, acquaintances, students, and clients in mind who have introduced themselves to me by saying, "I just love color!" Their exuberance for making meaningful color choices has inspired me to organize my thoughts about color's multifaceted complexity when seen outdoors. That acid green that jumped out at you on the rocky edge of the shoreline as the tide dropped . . . the periwinkle sky above a field of grasses bleached out by winter's wear . . . a bug with a gem-like iridescent teal body you've never seen but your ten-year-old son found in the woods this morning, recounting it with exuberance.

As you view, taste, touch, smell, and hear color from now on, *Nature of Color* can be left in your glove compartment or on the mudroom shelf to remind you to get back out there. Most of all, it will be a diary of what caused you on earlier outings to stop and examine an ecosystem with an intention to recognize color properties. From these experiences you will derive useful tools for shaping your world at home with an artist's assurance. Pulling the focus wider, I have no doubt that the more you see with all your senses and learn about the amazing things going on outside in the sunlight right under your nose, the more you will find incredible uses for color that will change the way you live, and protect and love nature.

CHAPTER I

YOUR VIEW

Let's face it—your vision isn't what it used to be. No matter how young or old you are, your view is ever-changing and you are becoming more discriminating each day. Every visual sighting requires you to respond either to the sunlit natural world or the artificial light of a built environment. Indoors, visibility is conditioned to keep nature at bay, the landscape's three-dimensional reality outside compressed by window frames. Stepping outside, you become immediately aware of the natural habitat where you live. Whether indoors or outdoors, you engage your five senses and cognitively construct memory. This input is stored in your brain until you apply it to a new experience. That is to say, your life history influences your sensory understanding of the natural world. This is where our field guide to color begins.

Your cache of color intelligence gathered from birth is like a garden. You've cultivated your plot of soil with visual experiences from a lifetime of wonder and experimentation, and they are growing. To get the most out of your crop of color knowledge, your perceptions need to be continually flexed, re-examined, weeded for accuracy, and then harvested to apply to everyday practice.

You train your "mind's eye" to work the way you think. When you go color exploring outside, you will see things in the landscape that will amaze you and later compel you to understand better. With *Nature of Color,* you will use color principles from physics, optics, human physiology, art history, and my own shared experiences of paying close attention to nature. You will also find new relevance in disciplines that you know well. By more deeply relating to the ways color works in nature, you will learn to predict with an artist's confidence in all activities involving color choices.

Natural Resource for Color

There are as many ways to perceive nature as there are individuals. Each time that I climb in the mountains with friends or take a walk along one of the woodland trails near my home with a family member, I notice the things they notice. It can be surprising what intrigues hiking companions, and I'm always excited to see something new or to learn what stands out to my trail-mate from the camouflage of greens and browns.

Children work full-time exploring, testing, and learning to navigate the environment. As adults, we sometimes forget to give ourselves space and opportunity to rediscover and refine our view. Unscripted time outdoors reintroduces you to local habitat, which is increasingly overshadowed by our contemporary, two-dimensional, virtual reality. An afternoon trip to the beach or a picnic dinner by the lake provides time to observe color spectacles leisurely and indirectly as weather, wildlife, and seasonal changes steal your attention. This gathering of visual cues from nature happens effortlessly and is shaped by the reaction of those around you. Another person's descriptive words will trigger your senses and focus your attention on things you may have otherwise missed. Everyone learns about color by communicating their ideas. So hit the nature trail with your family, friends, classmates, and colleagues. Observe together visual wonders that stand out in natural light and make color visually commanding.

By making time to watch, wonder, and exalt in nature's awesome display, you retool your perceptions of the visual light spectrum. Sunlight, which all humans experience throughout the daylight hours as they live and work, triggers your senses in relatable ways and can stimulate trail chat with color at its center. As the practice of seeing color becomes a shared passion, you will find a path of inquiry necessary to satisfy your growing curiosity about the most stunning examples of vegetation, animal life, and the awesome "light shows" that naturally occur where you roam.

To witness nature's best flourishes, you need to keep close watch of the growing season. I make calendar notes of when something special is likely to appear, such as the elusive lady slipper orchid. A walk in the woods with a friend turns into a fun hunt for the exotic purple hue. Wild areas that you explore are very different as the seasons unfold. Even a familiar path will pique your curiosity when you step out in search of new hues, especially when you share the adventure with friends and family who have not been there before.

I encourage you to use the exercises in *Nature of Color* to consider optical concepts either before going out on a hike or after, when you've noticed color that inspires you to search for explanations. The experiments you try out with pastels or Color-aid paper will engage your brain in working out the mechanics of what you see outside. Repeat the exercises more than once. Practice will improve your vision as well as your understanding of how to reconstruct with color that which was captivating at the source.

Used as a field notebook, *Nature of Color* provides a place to paint what you see with a color medium or to take notes on what you found fascinating. As you organize your own experiences for future reference, you can begin to use color in your creative toolbox. Your view will be tested each time you try to build with pigment what you witness in the environment. With *Nature of Color* in your backpack, you can challenge yourself to engage different areas of your brain while examining the complex world of color. This process stimulates a deep wonder that increases with every attempt. This is where inspiration starts.

Color intrigue found on the trail accumulates just like the precious specimens that may fill your window ledge or grace the breakfast table where they can be handled and examined. Nature's intricate details are there to admire again and again, once you make a habit of immersing yourself in local habitat. Along the way, you and your walking companions, young and old, will gain a better understanding of your personal views as you use the language of color to share your experiences. This will lead you to accumulate a treasure chest of sumptuous color memories that will stick with you.

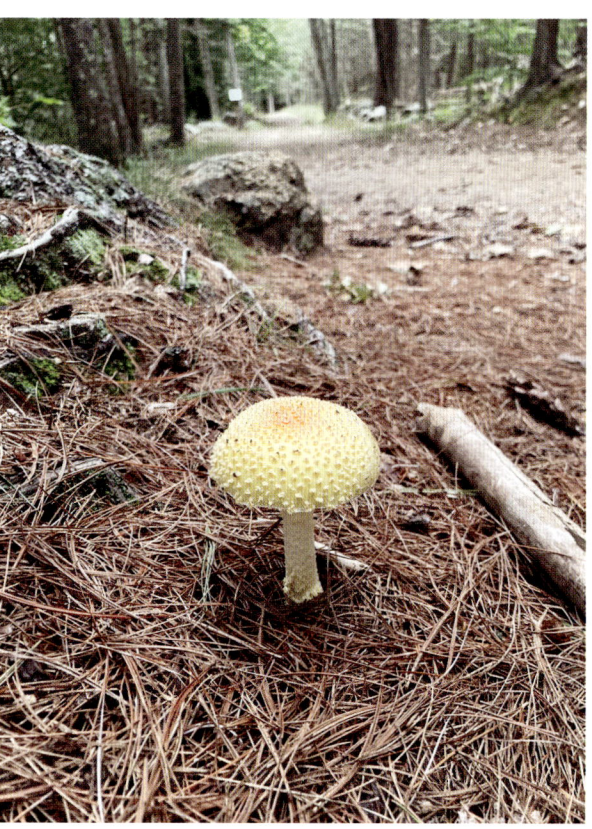

Ravenswood, Gloucester, MA

Seeing in Color

We detect sunlight as color using our frontal vision: taking in light through the lens in our eyes, stimulating the color sensitive cells of the retina, then transmitting the impulse from the synapse to the brain. Color registers in our consciousness immediately upon facing the subject of interest. Our first thoughts are the most accurate for identification. Keeping up with the speed of your vision is the name of the game with color. I recommend speaking aloud the color that you see as soon as your eyes land on the subject. Don't stop to think or the thought process will become addled.

When we see gray, or feel we do not understand what the color is that we are looking at, our rods and cones are telling us they need a rest. The perception of gray is confusion—all color receptors are firing together when we lose sight of the most powerful wavelength of light reflecting from the object in view. Looking away for a few seconds, then bringing focus back to the same spot will stimulate reception anew. Landscape painters use this trick to clear their vision. They also know from practice that color fatigue comes after intense focus of about twenty minutes, and it is best to create their painting schedule around these known physical limitations. Unfocused rest restores your eyesight and results in better color vision on the nature trail too. This can be as simple as removing one's eyeglasses for a couple of minutes, or looking out to a farther horizon before coming back to the closer subject at hand. If your *plein-air* painting is turning mud brown, you are likely fatigued. Take a walk and return with a fresh perspective!

You may be familiar with the assertion that men and women think different-ly, but did you know that males and females truly see differently? Females are often more sensitive to the experience of color, are aware of subtle nuances, and associate emotion to hue. Recently, a study of women with exceptional color vi-sion identified a chromosomal mutation that gives these females a fourth cone, contributing to the ability to see exponentially more colors in the spectrum of light than the average human. Males pay more attention to the value, the lightness or darkness of a color, relying on reception from their rods. They are more likely to experience color blindness, a condition that limits color perception. One student explained that her red/green color-blind husband needed to have family members identify spoiled food for him in the refrigerator.

Physiological color distinctions between the sexes become apparent when couples or families embark on a design project with an architect, interior designer, or color consultant. In an initial strategy session, it can be helpful for a couple to divide responsibilities based on each person's skills for the best outcomes, especially when it comes to color choices. For costly materials that will define the look of their home, this approach is very practical and can suit time constraints for getting work done. I believe with proper explanations of the physics of the site conditions, and knowing whose strengths lie where, a family can more easily accept the color-sensitive member's leadership in directing color choices. A skilled professional will ensure that all of the project stakeholders' personal desires are considered in a collaborative process. This negotiation of identifying each participant's strengths sometimes takes time, but the outcome is a color palette that pleases everyone's sense of home.

Over the many years that I have worked with students, clients, and home-owning couples, I've been attentive to ways people gracefully work around the obvious difference in color perception between the sexes and individuals. In class groups when students learn they are not seeing color in the same way as those around them, they begin to listen more intently to try and "see" what others do. I've noticed students' vision change through applying color theory and knowing better what to expect to see thanks to hearing from classmates. Finding a work-a-round is possible when you are aware of your limitations, keep an open mind, and apply what you know should be visible to you.

With more severe vision limitations, the path forward to greater color acuity relies more on trusting your eyesight to improve through continued training, even without experiencing immediate gratification. The brain has been shown to replicate cognitive function from a damaged part of the brain in another part of the organ in response to repeated stimulation. Seeing and speaking about color as you experience it reinforces your brain's cognitive response; you will improve your sensory perception and color memory with experience.

The adage "seeing is believing" acknowledges our preference to trust vision over other senses as we attempt to understand our world. We believe what we see with our own eyes, even when it is clear we are being deluded, as with a magic trick. "Believing is seeing"—this corollary conveys a trust in science, or what you know to be true. We have confidence that we can train our perception to have heightened sensitivity when the development of our color vision is supported by experience and facts. Just as any muscle that gets flexed and put to use, color perception improves with physical movement.

I have experienced my own vision improving with regular sessions of painting outdoors. I began using pastels to create nocturnes along the quiet road after dark, on the highway, and at industrial sites when I observed that nighttime simplified the grand landscape subject into a more color-focused image. I worked while my family slept. There were stunning color relationships in the dark, endlessly providing ideas for the next image. It was a challenge handling pastels in the dark, but I memorized their shapes and returned home with images that met my recollection of the experience. My night vision became so acute that I subconsciously began driving without headlights one night after a painting session. I was alerted to my error when I heard the honking of a frustrated driver coming along on the opposite side of the road—an occupational hazard of exceptional night vision!

On the Trail

People come in different physical shapes and sizes, and an individual's eye level influences what they notice along a trail. The angle of light that reflects from foliage can completely change the color that is perceived, just as the nap of a woven rug reveals either a light side or a dark one depending on the direction from which you view the surface. At an angle closer to the ground, children can notice quick moving snakes and fascinating miniature flora hugging the soil where they range. Children from cultures that share habitats with deadly reptiles are known to have a more astute sense of color as a result. Navigating your natural environment regularly gives you the power of keen observation and increases your relationship to color as it illuminates threats to be avoided.

Today, children are suffering developmental consequences from living their increasingly indoor lifestyle with limited unstructured time to revel in nature. Recent studies show that not spending enough time outdoors, negotiating the twists and turns of a wild habitat, has caused children to become gradually more anxious and their eyesight more myopic. Our vision is best trained in the irregularities of the natural world and becomes progressively more agile as we grow.

A child's proclivity to touch what she sees is precisely the investigative method one needs for a full exploration of color. For example, ferns have hidden seeds dotting the underside of their leaves in neat rows, which are sheltered from the sun-angled top that we view from above. The resulting color shift from top to bottom can be visible only when wind ruffles the fern bed or when a curious child takes fern in hand and sees for himself.

One way to prevent unhappy consequences from touching poisonous plants while hiking is to check the warnings for problematic vegetation at the trailhead

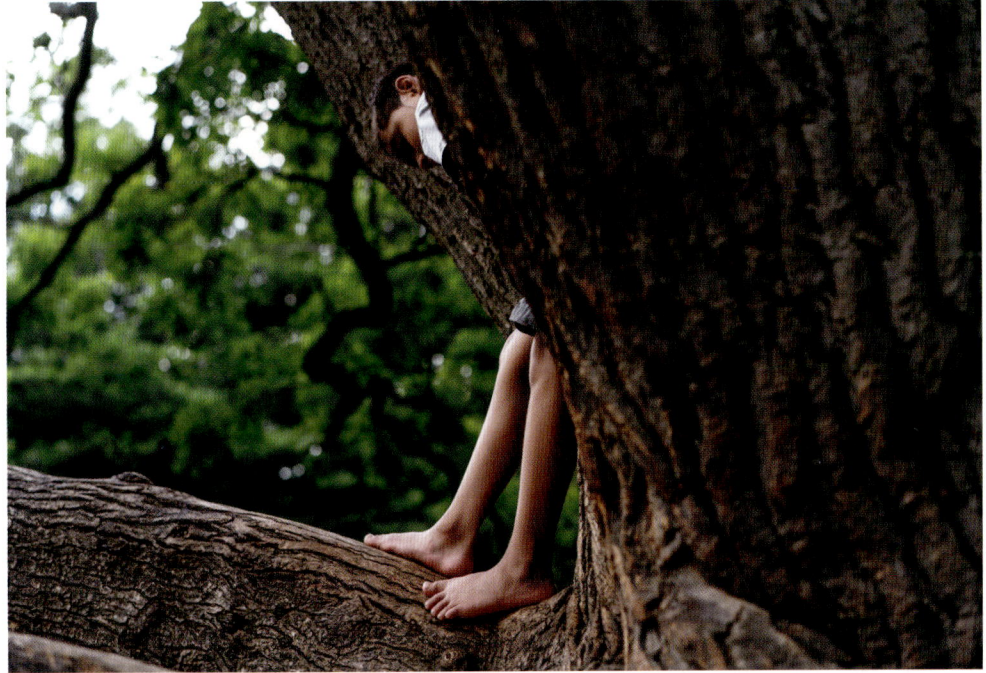

"A Slow Reveal," Felice Simon

before embarking on your hike. There you will find mug shots of the offending plants. When a trail sign is not readily available, research online or use a plant identification app to learn the conditions that allow poisonous flora to flourish.

Children are not the only inspiring explorers. Your canine companions can help lead you in your color adventures. When your dog vigorously wags his tail while inspecting things along the way, his enthusiasm expands your notion of what is compelling. Though a dog's color vision is limited, a need to sniff every inch of the path and follow every scent are exemplary study habits for learning how to search for color specimens.

Riding horses gives you a new angle for seeing nature and reaching vistas you may not have had access to otherwise. With their protective instincts, horses often step gently to avoid danger and sometimes respond skittishly to a snake-like stick or an ominous rock. This prey awareness of the horse can make the rider more conscious of every step so as not to miss out on color treasures along the way.

There is an important relational facet to working with color in art and design. Your ability to see through the lens of a trail-mate, noticing how color captures his or her attention and comparing it to your own, prepares you to discuss color in group projects, to design for a client's needs and wants, or to make art that moves the viewer. Exploring a trail with different companions provides a check on your internal light meter, helping you to understand where your personal view of color lands within the range of "normal."

Those who are reluctant to "talk color" may be less sensitive to color cues or unsure of what they are seeing. For this reason, all hikes should be planned to pursue personal interests, such as wildlife, geology, or even athletic endurance. When particular passions are taken into account, color curiosity will naturally ease into all shared observations. As in other human interactions, listening to someone else's perspective on the trail is as illuminating as volunteering your own.

Color provides a powerful message without words. Its overt visual impact has huge financial implications because of the value that we place on beauty. Get color right and humans will be drawn like insects to light. Because of this, color must meet the needs of the end user of architecture, graphic design, and other applications. For those designers or artists collaborating on projects, I recommend hiking with another colleague whom you work with regularly. This break from the two-dimensional indoors and flat screens could take the form of a lunchtime trail walk to explore color together.

I have experienced how this small, enjoyable effort supports refreshed eyesight and a more intuitive team approach, which builds on individual strengths for observing color. I climb mountains and hike local reservations with an architect I have known for many years in my role as a color consultant. She may be sick of hearing me exalt the power of "nature bathing," but our hikes naturally include identifying trail color, making comparisons, and seeing possibilities for bringing our observations from nature into current projects. Our exchanges on the trail have increased our creative momentum and our ability to support one another while problem-solving on the job.

Dreaming In Color

One of the most important influences on human sight is memory. Your lifetime of experiences has colored your world and dictates what you see as much as the light right in front of you physically stimulates your view. The ease with which optical illusions are successful points to our reliance on learned experience overriding reality. Many forensic psychologists could attest to the likelihood that you'd see a woman's face in the shadows on the moon in the photograph on the following page.

This interpretation is based on what you expected to see in your earliest childhood memories. The human face of a woman/mother is a default setting when the subject is hard to recognize, and this image takes advantage of that bias. It is difficult to actually compare our visual understandings with someone else's,

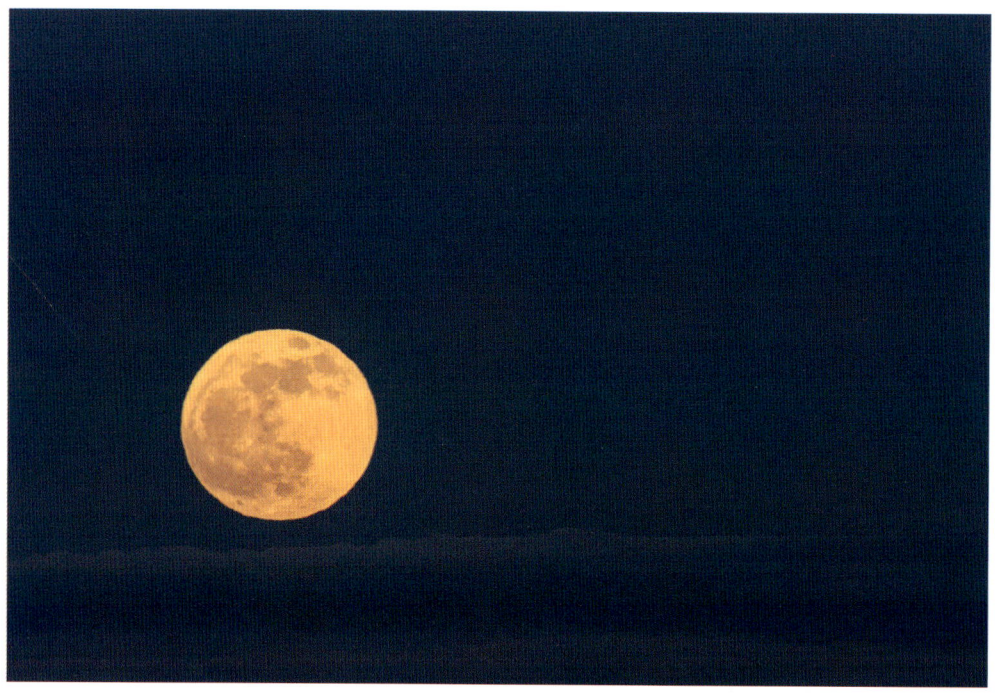

"Harvest Moon," Melissa Cox Photography

but it is essential to recognize that what we see may be distorted by our own personal history and culture. Some lifestyles and careers do not require one to empathize with what another person might be seeing or understanding, especially when different from what one expects to see themself. However, a creative artist who works well with others keeps implicit bias in mind and in check.

Savvy architects, designers, and visual artists look for cues from the project site's ecology that will create visual conditions—but they also listen for indicators in a client's language and notice personal expressions of color, such as choices previously made at the home or in what the client is wearing. Sleuthing subtle cues in conversation with fellow hikers will help you learn how color is understood, as well as misunderstood. This habit of trying to learn more about "where the other person is coming from" not only helps you connect with people; when continually practiced, it helps you to retain acute sensitivity. You will become aware that what you consider real and what others consider real are different because we project our own unique memories onto the color at hand.

Keeping in mind the significance of memory for shaping our vision, those who wish to work objectively with color in service to the general public must study the basics of cultural norms and of the physics of light. We know from observing newborns and young children that color vision is limited as we first emerge into the world. Our eyesight improves and our color vision becomes more nuanced as we explore and examine our first home environment. Primary colors are the most easily detected by developing eyesight. This is why we associate red, blue, and yellow as child-friendly colors. Secondary colors—orange, green, and purple—also stimulate a young child's vision when in saturated tones. Secondary colors are called "complementary colors" (also known as "opposite" colors), and they are the mixture of two primaries to create the color opposite the remaining primary (i.e., red and yellow makes orange, which is the complement of blue). As a child's vision improves with age and practice, more subtle hues attract their attention and inform their view. Our personal memory of encountering color as we have explored our world has filled our brain's "hard drive" with a detailed understanding of hue that our perception reactivates when we witness color anew.

As you become more sophisticated in your reaction to color on the trail, you will feel more than ever the physical well-being that comes when all your senses are taking in a beautiful landscape. Let your interpretations of how others are responding to breathtaking visuals guide you. This practice is the daily intention of the artist or designer using color in conversation to launch the imagination of their client into a full color sensory experience.

Color Vision Baseline

To judge how far away something is, the depth of a puddle, or the heat of a stovetop, we look for color to signal the information we need to make our next move. When your eyesight is intensely stimulated by a color to the state of fatigue, your vision automatically responds by projecting the opposite color onto a highly reflective/white ground. In the woods, that may be a paper birch trunk; at the ocean, the sunlit white sand or the white shirt of a sunbather.

Artists and designers use the concept of complementary colors to stimulate the viewer's natural reflex action, knowing the outcome will create an engaged response. It is no accident when an interior designer chooses orange for a pop of color in a cool blue or white room. Orange is the mixture of yellow and red, the complement to blue. In nature, you may look out to a sunny landscape with an intense blue sky stretching out above the horizon and notice an abundance of orange foliage and flowers; they are made more vibrant in the presence of a dominant primary.

Calibrating your internal color meter can begin with the following demonstration designed to test your natural color reflexes. Using the white page in *Nature of Color* as a background, place the green square (provided) or a green leaf from the trail in the center of the page and settle the field guide on the ground or on a rock in the sunshine. Focus your attention only on the green square or leaf and wait twenty seconds without moving your gaze from the color. Then remove the square/leaf and continue to look at the now blank, white page. What do you see? There will still be color projected onto the highly reflective white plane of light, but now it will be different. The stimulation of your reflexive eyesight is in response to being bombarded by green light. You will see a mirage of the same size square or leaf shape in the *opposite* or *complementary* color. This is your body's way of giving your vision a rest, activating the cones that are sensitive to the other two primaries, both at the same time.

In the field, the green of summertime foliage will barrage your vision in a woodland environment. The ocean's sky-reflecting surface presents cool greens, blues, and grays. Out west, in the canyons, on mesas, and along hill country paths, the arid red rock fills your field of vision with warm oranges, reds, and purples. Before you head into such highly colorful environments, check your vision for a reflexive response or a naturally occurring opposite: Focus on one of the provided squares of primary color. Test how your eyes respond to the color and how it projects the opposite color on any nearby surface of white. Then test each square and record your findings.

Color Expectations

Before your next planned hike, I recommend visiting the local paint store. Select eight colors that you expect to see in the natural environment from the paint chip display of colors available for home improvements. Cut all of the color samples into the same size square and paste them on one side of the page provided in this field guide. Add your own descriptive word or two next to each color square: acid green, calming blue, rock crystal blush, etc. Now head outside and look for examples of the colors that you anticipated. In a square next to the paint store color you expected to see, use your pastels to create the color that is closer to what you are actually seeing. How do your on-site examples vary from your paint store samples? What surprising variations of hue appear in full sunlight? Jot down your reflections on how nature's color reality differs from man-made color.

Now give color names to the pastel samples that you have created to tell the story of your hike. These names will be helpful for when you discuss or write down insights from that day's hike, specifically what you were finding versus what you anticipated. These may become color hypotheses, supported with experience over time—or, at the very least, a correction you can acknowledge of your baseline view from where you started your journey with this color field guide.

Note: Prismacolor Nupastels (24 box set) are an excellent color tool for this exercise. They are non-toxic pastels that can be layered to approximate the color that you see. Do not be afraid of building up color as you work. To darken a color, use the next darker, cooler color in the box rather than black. To lighten a color, use the lighter version in the box rather than adding white. If the green is not warm enough, add yellow. If the red is not deep or cool enough, add blue or purple.

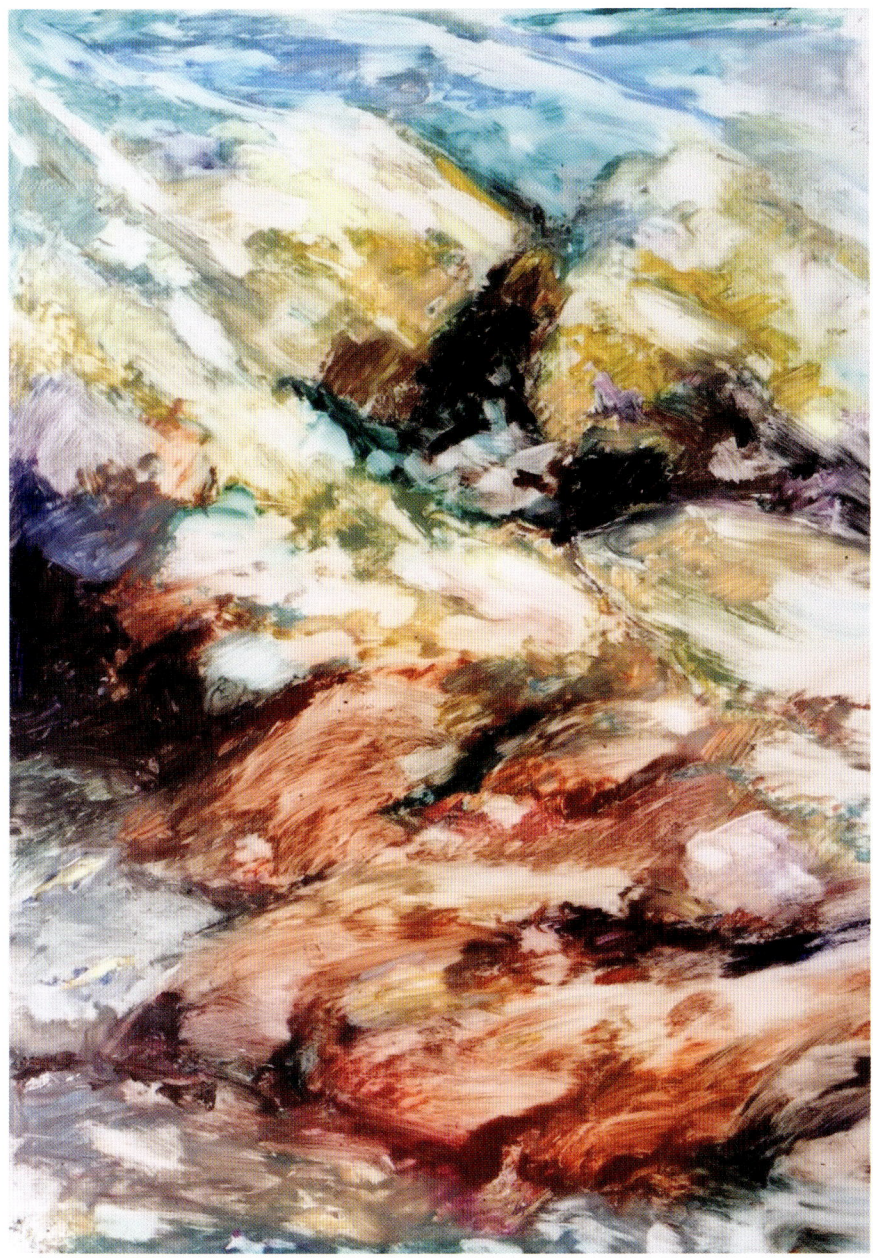

"Baia Da Barca Underwater," oil stick on YUPO paper, Pico Island, Azores

CHAPTER II

FIELD STUDY

What makes you curious about how sunlight works in the environment? What excites your imagination in nature? It takes some planning to figure out the answers. Your natural habitat is an unparalleled laboratory where you can begin your investigations of color. You must first initiate a new habit, or place value on an existing one, of getting out into nature regularly, especially when there isn't a well-worn path outside your door. To learn color principles that will change your view, reacquaint yourself with what was once your playground and can be again.

Our contemporary lives are for the most part lived within artificial atmospheres framed by man-made light sources and synthetic structures, as well as air, light, and sound pollution. Your quest to use color with three-dimensional impact begins when you consciously take leave of the built environment, which is designed to keep you at a safe distance from natural elements. If you are ready to take a closer look at what's going on in the wider world that speaks to your spirit, here are some tips on how to get there.

Dress For Success

This is not about fashion. To start exploring color in nature, you must consider what you will wear hiking and how clothing affects what you see. For a clear view in the wild, your eyes need to be undistracted by color in your peripheral vision. This is because color is contextual; we see one color in relation to all that surrounds it. A busy, colorful fabric will interfere with your vision.

As the most light reflective of colors, white is the best choice to wear on your upper body for an unobstructed view because it is all colors of the rainbow radiating together, providing a comparison that will be one of the least influential on your eyesight. A scientist's white lab coat is the ultimate attire for giving you an undistracted view of hue—though I can't recommend it purely on style! Highly illuminated, white will also keep you cool if you are hiking on a hot day and want to shed the sun's heated rays. It can also reveal unwanted tagalongs, like ticks, that get picked up as you trek.

Black and navy are colors that absorb light and will stand distinct from the natural landscape. In the light of the sun, black is not a natural color of the land or vegetation. You may think you see black as you scan a scenic landscape, but upon closer inspection you will find these to be dark versions of blues, browns, reds, and purples. Black and navy can also dampen the glare of harsh light and offer a contrast to what you are inspecting.

If you find that you will be hiking in an area where hunters could be in transit, by all means designate someone in your trail group to wear "international orange" or another luminous color on their backpack or as a hat. However, the person wearing orange should hang to the back to avoid influencing the others' vision. The day-glow intensity will not infringe on the wearer's eyesight and will provide maximum safety.

Dress to be comfortable for predicted weather, for the amount of exertion, and for trail conditions. Your first-light clothing choices will influence your level of ease outdoors for the entire day. Think of clothing as protecting our bodies the same way shelter does. A thoughtful selection of what to wear outdoors is a priority for making the most out of your play time.

Sunglasses are one of the first accessories to go with us when we head outside. They provide our eyes with protection from UV light, insects, and chance encounters with sticks. Additionally, they greatly reduce visual fatigue, especially on water, snow, and ice. Despite all of the important protections that sunglasses provide for our vision, color acuity is increased when sunglasses are left in your pocket as you begin your adventures. If you are worried about visual fatigue on the trail, a hat can offer shade and impact color vision less.

To make it easy to pick up and go, I suggest having ready at all times a designated backpack to hold exclusively your pastels or water-soluble crayons, a small-handled watercolor brush, hand wipes, water, a collapsible water holder, first-aid, sunscreen, a hat, a neck gaiter, bug spray, a headlamp, and your copy of *Nature of Color*. You may want to paint what inspires you or try out a recommended color experiment when you've found a place to rest and eat lunch, all the while taking advantage of free-thinking opportunities in real time. What moves you is fleeting. Prepare ahead for nature-trail wonders and you won't miss them!

Local Color

"Seeing" more nature requires that it is accessible and local. Thankfully, no matter where you live, open space and scenic landscapes are prized features, even in big cities. From Central Park in New York City to Golden Gate Park in San Francisco, parks are there for all to enjoy: children with outdoor-motivated teachers, salary workers hoping to make the most of lunch hour, families spending time together on weekends, and tourists who visit year round. More and more cities, towns, and neighborhoods are becoming known for their conserved landscapes as communities have sought to preserve their undeveloped areas for the enjoyment of future generations. Start with these public reserves where you can get to know the trails on your own terms. Use your appointed exercise time to speed walk or run a coastal path where you know the mileage. Before you go, make a pact with yourself that you will stop and inspect color you might have otherwise run past.

If nature reserves and parks are not near your urban community, start exploring your skyscape: the light that illuminates clouds in weather systems overhead or the atmospheric color unique to patterns of climate where you live. Get to know public high-rises with the best views so you can make regular visits to chronicle the sky above.

Color observatories can even begin in your own backyard with home gardens, which move ever closer toward wilderness despite best intentions. A gardener's wisdom is inspired by the land and the amount of unfettered time they spend there weeding on their knees, planting new seeds, pruning, and harvesting. It is hard work, but for the passionate gardener, it hardly seems so as the garden is a playground for endlessly enjoying the magic of color and nature's insistence.

You can get out onto the water easily in rowboats, kayaks, and canoes, all under your own power. This makes for quiet, contemplative observation, but unless you can anchor, it may be a little tricky to stay in one place for painting. Even so, boating along a coastline, down a river, or on a local lake puts you in touch with the systems that control our planet's marine and aquatic environments. These experiences generate endless opportunities to explore the fascinating color of the water world, so it is worthwhile to find a medium that suits your boat's motion.

Local color is the term used to explain the appearance of color that is next to the viewer when describing the concept of *color perspective* (hue as it appears in three dimension). When we see color next to us, or hold it in our hand as a sample, a common misconception is that the color is static. In reality, color varies with every movement of the light that illuminates the surface of an object. It also changes in context to everything that is around it: the color of our skin, the clothing we are wearing, or the color of the floor we are standing on. For example, when we look at someone next to us, we will see the person wearing a particular color, but when that person moves farther away, let's say across an expansive lawn, we will see the color of the clothing change because water molecules in the air make the color bluer and grayer and less defined.

There are other ways that the brain distorts our perception of color. In passive mode, people often generalize color in order to keep it in their awareness. To be proactive with color, you instead must convince yourself that context is everything. Forget about taking a friend's paint chip for her dining room and handing it off to your painter for your living room. It will never, could never, work in the way you saw it and liked it at her home! Only by sampling your friend's color in the light of your living room will you learn if it will have the same look where you want to put it and for the activities you hope to inspire there.

See for Yourself

We see color with our frontal vision. Our eyes see and then our brains understand color in seconds. This very notion is important to work into your color practice. It takes only a movement, or a quick comparison to another color, such as white, to make the most accurate assessment with our eyes. *Nature of Color* provides blank white drawing paper to be used as a backdrop to see color more accurately on the trail, as well as for filling with notes and drawings. You will soon be convinced that context dictates what you see, and how helpful it is to have some kind of white material on hand when you scout for color.

TRY THIS AT HOME

Materials: white paper, three objects of same hue

On a white piece of paper, line up three small objects of the same hue, though not alike. Take the darkest one away. What happens to the color of the two remaining objects? How would you describe each color? Write down adjectives to express what you are seeing. Now, take the same three objects and replace the darkest item with something black. Say out loud what has happened to the two remaining objects. Do you notice any new tones that were not visible before? (For the record: Take a photo with your phone of the objects on the white paper to revisit the example again another time and see/record what you think.)

TRY THIS ON THE TRAIL

Materials: *Nature of Color*

On your next hike, gather three leaves from different plants along your walk. Place the three specimens on the white page in *Nature of Color*. Take the darkest away and say out loud what has happened to the other two specimens. Now replace the darkest leaf of the remaining pair and say out loud what has occurred, being specific about any tonal changes. Place something black along the trail's edge and see what happens to the foliage that is now its context. Is black a standout? Does it blend with the foliage? (For the record: Take a photo with your phone of the objects on the white paper to revisit the example again another time and see/record what you think.)

CAUTION: When you first arrive at the location of your hike, take a look at the sign posted at the trailhead to identify the poisonous plants in the immediate area.

Color in Context

The following visual experiments give you an opportunity to test how humans view color through comparison, recording the light of the world in their consciousness with the darkest color only as dark as the other objects are lighter.

TRY THIS AT HOME

Take an object, put it in the sunlight of a window, and take note of what has happened to the color. Now quickly remove it from the window light and place it in a shadow. How has the move away from the sunlight changed what you see? Write down your impressions.

TRY THIS ON THE TRAIL

Place the darkest leaf from your collection into the full sun on the path and take note of the color. From the full sun, now move the same leaf to the shade near your place on the trail. What has happened to its color?

Found Color

Where do you begin an exploration of color in nature when there are so many amazing views to draw your attention and stimulate your passion for hue? I suggest looking for examples of local color in the berries that you find on a bush beside you or the seaweed at the beginning of the descent into the intertidal zone of the sea. Found Color borrows from the artist tradition of taking something found (AKA "Found Object") and using it to inspire and inform or to be used as a material element in a current art creation.

Taking Pictures

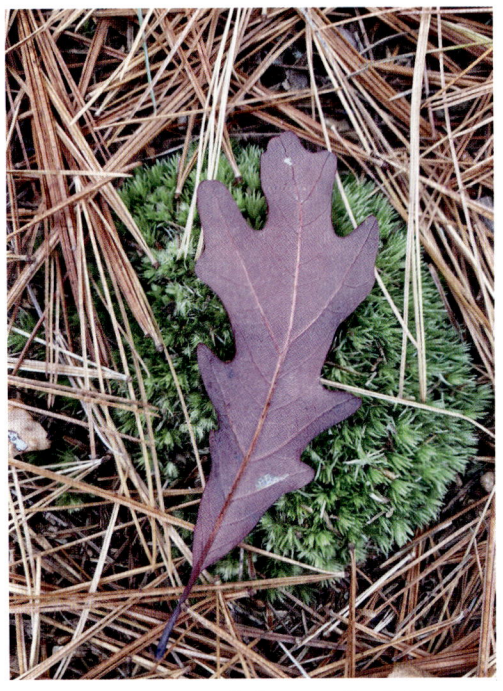

Beverly Commons, Beverly Farms, MA

Let your trail mates or beach-combing family lead a hunt for Found Color. Using your phone, snap pictures of anything of interest: any color, vibrancy, or detail. You don't even need to know what it is. With each framed example, study more closely the characteristics of the color and why it caught your attention.

Make a habit of scavenging as you move through nature. Narrow down your interests by framing them with the camera, then share the images with your friends and followers on Instagram. Snap something colorful on the trail that you think your friends would find unusual—that yellow capped mushroom that got everyone oohing and aahing, or maybe the lichens on a stone that appear uniquely blue when other specimens are more yellow or green. Such a visual scavenger hunt can become a fun habit of framing and sharing images of what you find curious along the trail. I guarantee you will keep finding ever more unusual colors and curious details once you start looking and using your camera's "viewfinder" to focus your attention on discoveries.

Photo Color

The camera is an important first tool for jump-starting the habit of asking questions about what you see firsthand in nature. As an image-recording device, your cell phone camera is invaluable because it conveniently produces visual high points and linear details. However, photographic color is still nothing more than a close approximation to what you saw in nature using all of your five senses. Human experience of being in nature does not limit itself to what the camera lens detects. Photos represent color at one instance of light in a facsimile of color relationships, fixed in an artificial two-dimension format. A snapshot does not replicate what we "see" in the world we explore unaided.

Our contemporary world is comprehensively illustrated by color photography. Images of everything on earth prime our vision with the "look" of a subject before seeing it for ourselves. It is impossible to avoid having visual expectations. "Eye candy" stokes our curiosity to catch sight of what we imagine exists out there in the wild, evoked by a photograph or film. True to the reference to candy as a short-lived pleasure, for many, color in nature pales in comparison to the vivid promotional photo version that originally aroused the allure.

Still, there is no substitute for seeing color in real time and three-dimensional space. Photography captures what you see minus the humid breeze that blows through your hair, the smell unique to the earth as you step along, and the thrill of discovery in your widening eyes. A photo cannot remind your color receptors later to stimulate your brain in the same way that a painting or collage you have constructed on location triggers the memory of your other senses. Your effort to build color relationships that you see in nature, painting what is before you, leaves an indelible imprint on your brain, right where it will feed future creative ideas.

The nineteenth-century assumption that the human eye worked similarly to a camera actually did not account for what we know today is a key component of sight. Memory of things seen in our past informs our perceptions too. Nineteenth century painters embarked on a tradition of working in nature and there discovered the value of learning from the landscape. Luminist painters such as Fitz Henry Lane, Martin Johnson Heade, Albert Bierstadt, and many more ushered in an American era of painting the magnificence of the landscape. Nowhere before had artists captured nature's awe-inspiring vistas of the wild American landscape in pictures. This landscape tradition continues to influence painting in the twenty-first century, challenging the artist's vision and view of color that can make illusions of space and sunlight possible.

Picture Making

Nature of Color provides you with a viewfinder that works just like the one in your camera to define the picture plane (see page 158). This paper cut-out can help you focus your vision in the practice of making picture compositions along the trail amid the great expanse of the outdoors. Limiting your view, close one eye and look through the cut-out rectangle horizontally, for a landscape composition, or vertically, for a portrait composition. The page can be cut out of the book, or you can fold all other pages to one side, holding it about 6 inches from your face. Framing picture ideas in this way will teach you to select subjects from what you are seeing, which can be explored in a color study painted with more control.

You are not always prepared to take out pastels or another painting tool when you want to record color that interests you on an outing. I recommend writing descriptive words about what you are witnessing on location when painting is not possible. Words can define the quality of color that inspired your interest, helping to imprint the memory while you struggle to connect the sensation of the light reflected. Drawing comparisons to food and recalling tastes, touch, and sounds that reflect the kind of color that appears in your field of vision will allow you to read the words later and fine-tune your impression of the color again.

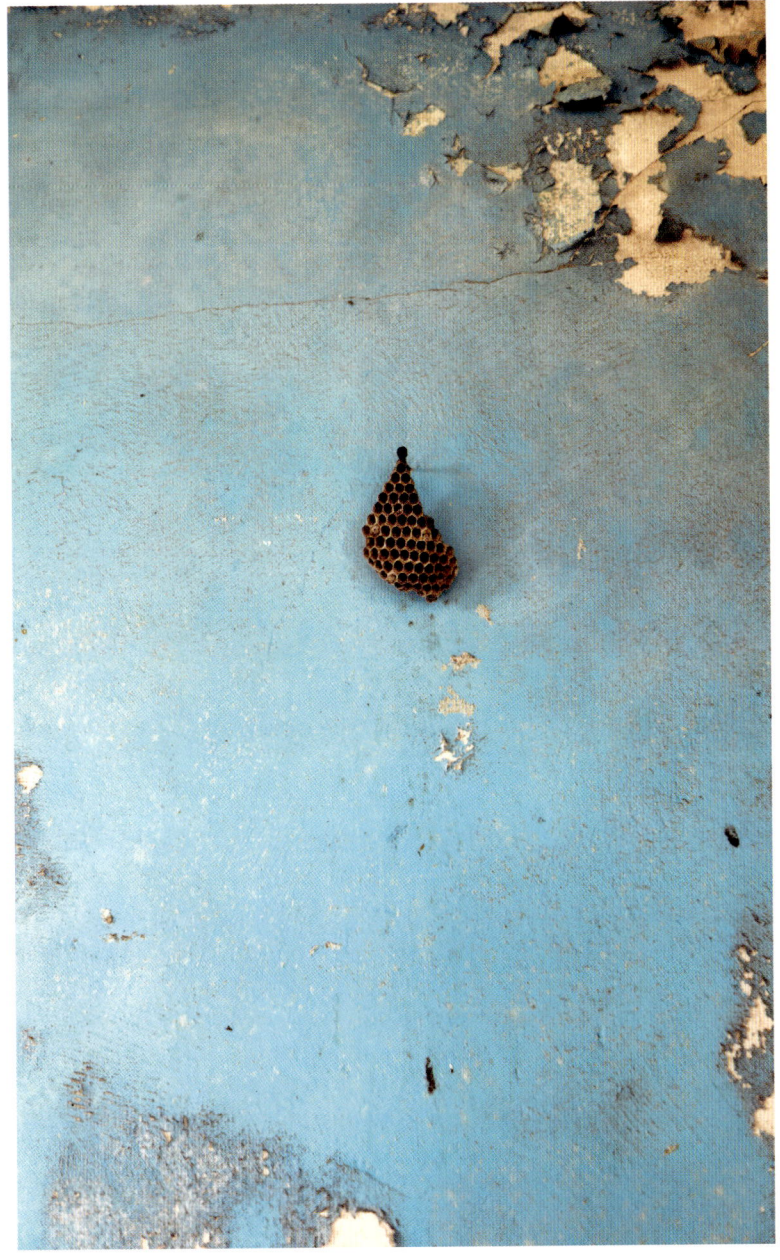

"Jack Spaniard," Nadia Huggins

CHAPTER III

HIKE

Escaping into nature on a hike is a full-body breakout from your daily routine. Fortunately, getting outside regularly is beneficial to our physical wellbeing. Habitual nature excursions also reduce stress-induced conditions, such as anxiety and depression, and are good for visual health as well. Scouting out of doors stretches our eye muscles and greatly matures our perception.

Take any trail into nature and immediately your feet must make adjustments over ground that undulates and changes from the results of weather, tide, watertable, plant growth and decay, as well as the obstacles of an untamed ecosystem. The vastly increased scale of the environment laid out before you radically changes your awareness. You are now seeing, feeling, smelling, hearing, and touching the landscape that unfolds as you walk. It is impossible to take in all the sights and sensory input at the same time and you must fine-tune your movements to be fluid with the world being out of square. Leave the phone in your pocket and soak in the sights that are accompanied by smells of earth and sounds of your footfalls on the geology that stretches out ahead of your ramble.

We belong there in the woods, valleys, marshes, and oceans, on the mountains and at the beaches, but we must try to be cognizant of the creatures that will sleep there at night. Our footprints, due to our numbers, have shown us that our presence can be damaging and, in some cases, irreversible. Sharpening perceptions and refining our planning capabilities with new understandings makes a relationship with nature good for both of us. Be mindful of the game trail that is visible through the underbrush. Stick to trails for hiking and mountain biking in respect of the landscape that gets rutted as we pass. Make sure that your choice of access to the beach does not crush the fragile beach grass stabilizing the dunes or disrupt nesting shorebirds. Watch where you tread, but cherish the learning as a sacred trust that nature has provided. The more you go, the more you know.

Weather Eye

Weather in your area responds to geography, the influence of aquatic and marine systems, prevailing winds, and other known patterns. Safely navigating conditions is a skill that needs to become second nature in guiding continued explorations at home and preparing you for adventures further afield. If you don't already follow the weather on an application that has radar and daily and hourly predictions, start a fascinating new habit that will aid planning your outings. Before setting out on a hike, be sure to look at a weather model and plan your experience as much as humanly possible. A visual image from the radar will show you how the current local system will affect your plans.

"Keep a weather eye." Sage advice, but it takes practice to do just that. Terrain or water intelligence comes in small incremental lessons, illuminated by nuanced sights and sensations that only experience can make real to us. Risk is inherent to exploring the land and sea, but self-confidence will reward those who make nature expeditions on a regular basis. For example, as children, my brother and I learned that our parents' encouragement to explore our summer environment—on Ipswich Bay—was supported by adages to offer guidance, but these were simply not reinforced by their own experience. Our parents lovingly provided boats, swimming lessons, lifejackets, and well-wishes, but we took it upon ourselves to get back alive from our ocean adventures using caution and our developing maritime savvy. After a few frightening mishaps, we regrouped and continued researching and skill building during the off season. By example, we passed our wisdom in a family chain of knowledge to younger siblings and, years later, to our own children.

The view overhead accompanies all outdoor adventure. Cloud profiles and the associated weather systems generating their formation is intel invaluable to the hiker and nature enthusiast. Clouds are huge moving water features in the sky influencing what we see from the ground up. They are a part of a larger cinematic view of the air streams transporting weather and color conditions to your location. The sun's path will light up the vaporized water, producing sculptural light-forms, billowing aloft from super-heated air composed of highly reflective water molecules. A drop in temperature will cause the water to condense and the clouds to thicken, creating darker colors of deep blues, grays, and purples. Then comes the rain. The sky-light view above places you at the center of a gigantic waterworks.

There is a progression to the visual characteristics of clouds building across a clear blue sky and messaging a premonition of coming weather. Rhythmic swoops of feathery clouds known as "mare's tails" or the fish-skin patterned "mackerel scales" in the upper atmosphere suggest a warm front arriving with rain and changing winds. On a moonlit night, a mackerel sky's silvery fish scales are chased across the metallic blue-gray of the night ending in an overcast start to the day. The clouds over your head are as good a predictor of weather as any hourly report. As you become a more involved observer of clouds, you will be able to read an open horizon and sense the wind speed moving the frontal system along, as well as temperature changes to come. You will be able to outrun weather that looks messy, adjust the timing of an outdoor activity, or wait out a change that is more to your liking.

The setting sun's fiery red is more than a romantic end to the day. "Red at night, sailor's delight" refers to the departing weather system illuminated by the setting sun, foretelling of a rising barometer of high pressure and clear skies. Conversely, waking to an early morning glow of pink portends the cloud cover of a storm approaching: "Red in the morning, sailor's take warning." Certainly take warning from a mariner's wisdom, then see for yourself what it means when the color red, the longest wavelength of light, is refracted from the water molecules of dense clouds at the horizon.

That weather is hard to predict never changes. However, while teaching a landscape painting class outside every Monday throughout the seasons for eleven years, I noticed that weather stuck very closely to a seven-day pattern. Whatever it did one Monday, it would repeat on the next Monday, and for a couple of Mondays thereafter, until it moved into a new weather system (each of which lasted about three days) progressing to a new season. This observable pattern allowed me to plan my classes with a little more confidence, though I still expected to be occasionally surprised by a downpour, snow, or the happiness of parting skies revealing sunshine. I've learned to always have an alternative route out of the wind or to plan a better time-of-day option. Most helpful is to dress for the inevitable changes of weather. As Alfred Wainwright said, "There is no such thing as bad weather, just unsuitable clothes."

Color intelligence from years of watching and then applying conjectured color choices to paper or panels has allowed me to keep up with the building process required to recreate a vision at the speed of light. Color is best understood and juggled with context using your speediest application. Pastels are one of the best mediums to work out the color in the landscape that is a moving train of relationships. Take out your viewfinder, or shape your hands in a rectangle, to decide the image that will fill the rectangular shape of your paper. Then start laying down the colored passages that will recreate the space stretching out in front of you. To give structure to your view of the landscape, use a neutral color like gray or Naples yellow to point out large features within the boundary of the picture plan. Then work with the speed of someone who knows that this view will be taken away in a flash!

Stop to Observe

What can taking a walk in the woods accomplish when faced with the need to select colors for a building's exterior design or to predict a color outcome of any sort? Roving outside with nature at every viewing level, from the dirt at your feet to the sky above, may seem aimless. On the contrary, when repeated over time, this practice develops your sophisticated prowess of visual sorting.

You don't need to swim or snorkel where you walk along the coast each day to see where ocean creatures thrive hidden under the water's surface. The dark patch of water is not a shadow under a cloud. That fishy smell in the air is the aftermath of a feast. Scavenging birds follow fishing boats, while more discriminating waterfowl work the surface of a visible roil, the result of a large school of fish shattering the stillness. As a predator, you will sharpen your languishing hunting skills in the wild watching the goings-on of hungry creatures. Not to capture your prey, but to regain the spatial awareness that comes from using your stalking skills to notice color's subtle shifts.

Ever wonder why hunters have different colored camouflage attire for the same area that they prowl all year? Seasonal changes in color are significant enough that those wishing to remain hidden from prey must adjust their wardrobe for the highly trained eyesight of the locals. The woodland and shore loses its vibrant sunlit foliage with winter's dormancy and the low angle of the sun. During the spring you can expect to see the distinct orange and black of orioles hovering in circles over an early spring flowering quince, or hummingbirds furiously fluttering just above any red flower during summer, or catch sight of seals when you spot a deep charcoal shadow on fall's changing water color, then observe the head of the mammal that breaks the surface for air. Hiking and other outdoor activities immerse you in seasonal hue. Thereafter, you will have your own experienced notion of recurring color from encounters that you will never forget.

Color Eye

Old-school nature navigating rewards your color imagination with knowledge otherwise pocketed by your GPS. A walk in the park requires only the visual routing equivalent of a whale spy-hopping its way down the coastline. But take a mountain hike to the summit and you will need to orient yourself to the compass rose to maintain a well-planned vision of the travel beyond your view, which will take hidden twists and turns. Rehearse the trail map, committing its shape to memory: the lefts, the rights, change in elevation, and most importantly, the color of the blaze marking the trail that you can expect to find on trees and rocks, flagging your progress. Your phone has a compass that will come in handy for stopping to check your direction. Small, pin-on compasses are a great way for children to keep in touch with their direction in the woods, where getting a view of the sun is more difficult. Pin these on the top of mittens and your child will be fascinated by the gimbaled movement and the guiding support on the trek.

You are strengthening your visual color imagination when you layer your study of maps, orienteering towards magnetic direction, and relating everything to the sun's progress overhead. Color is sunlight illuminating the landscape up ahead. Anticipating the trail draws on a set of skills that will develop your capacity for spatial awareness, your sense of direction, and the ability of your mind's-eye to imagine color in relief. You could have the GPS do this for you and then store the memory of the task, but you will have lost out on the spatial training exercise of the adventure committed to your memory. If your goal is, for example, to imagine color for architecture with given site conditions, you will want to learn to navigate the old-fashioned way. Gaining spatial bearings allows you to intuit better what happens outdoors under the sun. This also sharpens your personal color sense and your ability to shape a successful vision for a building.

Your internal photometer is getting flexed unconsciously as you hike. For example, you avoid muddy areas that from a distance are darker than those of the surrounding earth due to their saturation with rainwater. You determine a tidepool looks passable because of the light color of the water. You make a quick inspection of a natural stone bridge across a stream. It appears to be dry, not green with algae that would make the rocks treacherous. These are color indicators that you have collected in your brain's library of hue from your young explorations that will serve you well to identify and mix color that you see before you.

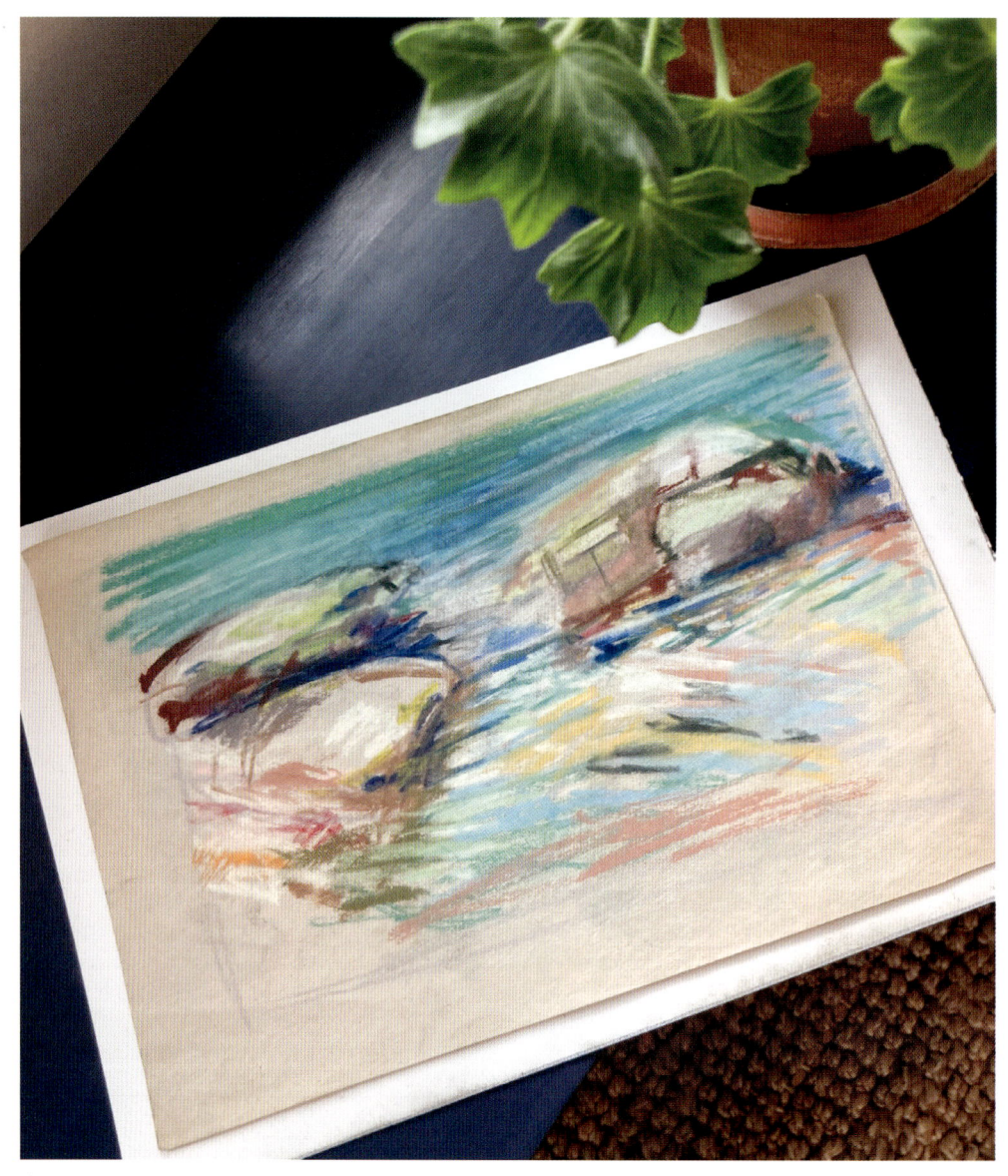

Prismacolor pastel study on paper

TRY THIS ON THE TRAIL

Materials: *Nature of Color*, pastels or oil sticks

Any free time on your hike that allows you to quickly use a color medium like pastels or oil sticks will refine your vision while also making note of a color of interest in your field journal pages. Don't be concerned if you do not have a large palette to work with or lots of time to spend. An important process in seeing color is discerning nuanced tones that make up what you see within the context of your medium's range of color.

You can explore a single local color by mixing the pigments of a limited box of pastels to achieve what you sense is right before you. Start with a pastel in a hue that closely approximates what you see, then find a paler color like that of the light on the surface of your specimen and use it first. You may have stopped to examine foliage. A green can be more yellow or even light blue. Start here and adjust by adding darker pigments to your first layer of hue. As you work, ask yourself if the leaf's color is warm or cool? How might the color taste or smell? Select your pigments to achieve these sensations. Don't be afraid of layering the color in your effort to get to what you see. Pastel can be overlaid and the pigments mixed or whisked away with a stiff paint brush when the color goes wrong. If oil stick is your preferred medium, you can bring a small palette knife with you and scrape away the waxy crayon that is not to your liking.

Knowing that color is context, you must also immediately see and fill in the colors that surround the subject that caught your attention. It is important to remember that color relationships within the limits of your box of pigments is what counts, not achieving the perfect match. This experiment with color on the trail will help you discover where you can go with your palette's range to create the scale of your sample, using darks and lights, warms and cools, or greener and browner colors.

A quick study of a hue can help you establish a general palette for the ecosystem where you hike regularly, preparing you to spend a little more time creating a larger, more encompassing landscape painting of color relationships on another outing. In your *Nature of Color* field guide, collect these color samples and mark them with date, time, weather, and location. Your collection of color specimens will record your internal library. This color vocabulary will be valuable to gaining greater speed in your future opportunities to work with color on location.

Color Perspective

From our earliest visual experiences, we've learned to adjust our thinking about the actual size of something that we see in the distance out-of-doors. The house at the edge of the field becomes larger as you walk towards it, though you and the house are not changing in size. Viewing a race of sailboats from the shore, you know in reality they are larger than the toy boat models they appear to be along the horizon. Your spatial certainty is reinforced when you walk down to the dock to meet the boats as they arrive and tie up after the day's race.

The reason for these illusions that inform our perspective is taught in drawing class: *linear perspective* explains how the lenses in our eyes distort the dimension of seen elements in the landscape in relation to where we are. We can draw and visually predict with line the angle of this distortion to replicate the human view of spatial reality. Lesser known, but equally impactful on what we see, is how color changes with light bouncing off of objects, visibly changing our view due to light refraction with depth. By practicing the basics of color perspective in the landscape where it is most easily seen, you will acquire one of the handiest tools for manipulating how color is perceived in three-dimensional space.

On location, I juggle the requirements of the terrain unaided—a free-climb, if you will. The experience of witnessing and reconstructing the color planes of the challenge posed by nature will develop your spatial color acumen in ways that duplicating the linear and color perspective information of a photo will not. The act of assembling the visual data of a full-scale landscape onto the painter's ground (paper, canvas, etc.) establishes the necessary cognitive pathways of the brain for skill building.

At the same time that the nineteenth century invention of the camera freed those pursuing portraiture and journalistic documentation to work outside, painters escaped to the countryside to explore nature, eager to try out emerging optical ideas about perception shared between scientists and artists of the day. These painters came to value the human sensory experience of being outside, and they bravely began setting up easels to paint in the open air to find color subtleties unrecorded on the black-and-white film of the current technology. Pioneering on-site painting was a way for these artists to advance past the restrictions of studio painting, as well as the traditional academic training that lent itself to a preordained outcome.

As part of their evolving personal reinvention of what is a painting, many nineteenth century artists were also exploring the science of human perceptions. One post-impressionist painter, Georges-Pierre Seurat, became particularly taken with the color theory literature of the time, especially the writings of Michel Eugéne Chevreul. Seurat began to develop a technique of applying fractured color for perceptual effects, which became known as *chromoluminarism*. A more refined method of using small dots of paint, known as Pointillism, evolved over time into Seurat's signature style of paint application. In the landscape, the nineteenth century painter used what to our contemporary eyes looks like pixelation. He encouraged the viewer to have a physical sensation while seeing the broken surface of small passages of color combinations. Triggered by the interplay of primary hues and their complements, the sensation created an optical tug-of-war. All cones of the viewer's eyes were being stimulated at the same time, while simultaneously the viewer experienced the harmony of small dots of opposing paint magically resulting in a perceived mixed color.

Another French painter benefiting from the contemporary science explored by the Impressionists was Paul Cézanne. He took the optical ideas of the day and created roughly hewn images of Mont Sainte-Victoire and other natural landscapes of his birthplace. These images looked unfinished to the public, who were more accustomed to studio devices for portraying the environment, and were roundly rejected by the established art world. However, Cézanne realized that the experience of his "unfinished" images could motivate the viewer to actively participate in seeing nature in its most authentic display. In building an image using color perspective principles, Cézanne's architectural approach honors the perceptual engagement of the viewer.

You can strive to model this same combination of artistic skill and respect for your viewer's involvement, especially as you use *Nature of Color* exercises to strengthen your insights for illusion. With this greater understanding of color perspective and a steady practice, you will work at a speed that matches your brain's fresh perceptions of a natural subject.

At first, though, the idea of painting the environment that you have stopped to enjoy may be overwhelming. The panorama, with its vast proportions illuminated by the speeding progression of changing light, cannot simply be "copied" onto a paper or canvas to recreate the scene. The French landscape painters of the nineteenth century would agree that the methodical approach of the studio (the Studio Chiaroscuro technique) just can't keep pace with the unique nuances of natural light and the rapidly changing color scene. In the unsuitable studio approach, you would start by carefully making a black-and-white line drawing of the landscape's features. Once you've established values, you then painstakingly match the color that you see starting on one end of the picture plane and adding successive colors. If you employ this labored technique outside during rapidly changing light conditions, your eyes and brain will become fatigued and your color choices will suffer, potentially lacking the fresh perspective of your first impressions.

Recognize, instead, that outdoor color is fluid and requires a more rapid process. Quickly mark the horizon, the major shapes of color, and a few key features with a light gray or dull orange. Simple strategies such as these can give you all the structure you need to begin the juggling act required to compete with the speed of daylight.

Here's How Color Perspective Works

Aerial perspective, the original term for color perspective, was first explored by nineteenth century Impressionist painters before the advent of the airplane. It allows an artist or designer to make quick, accurate color estimations using the physics of light. For instance, Cézanne understood that quickly painting the planes of color in relation to space builds volume, giving a viewer the structural information to articulate and see the site for themselves. This method prioritizes

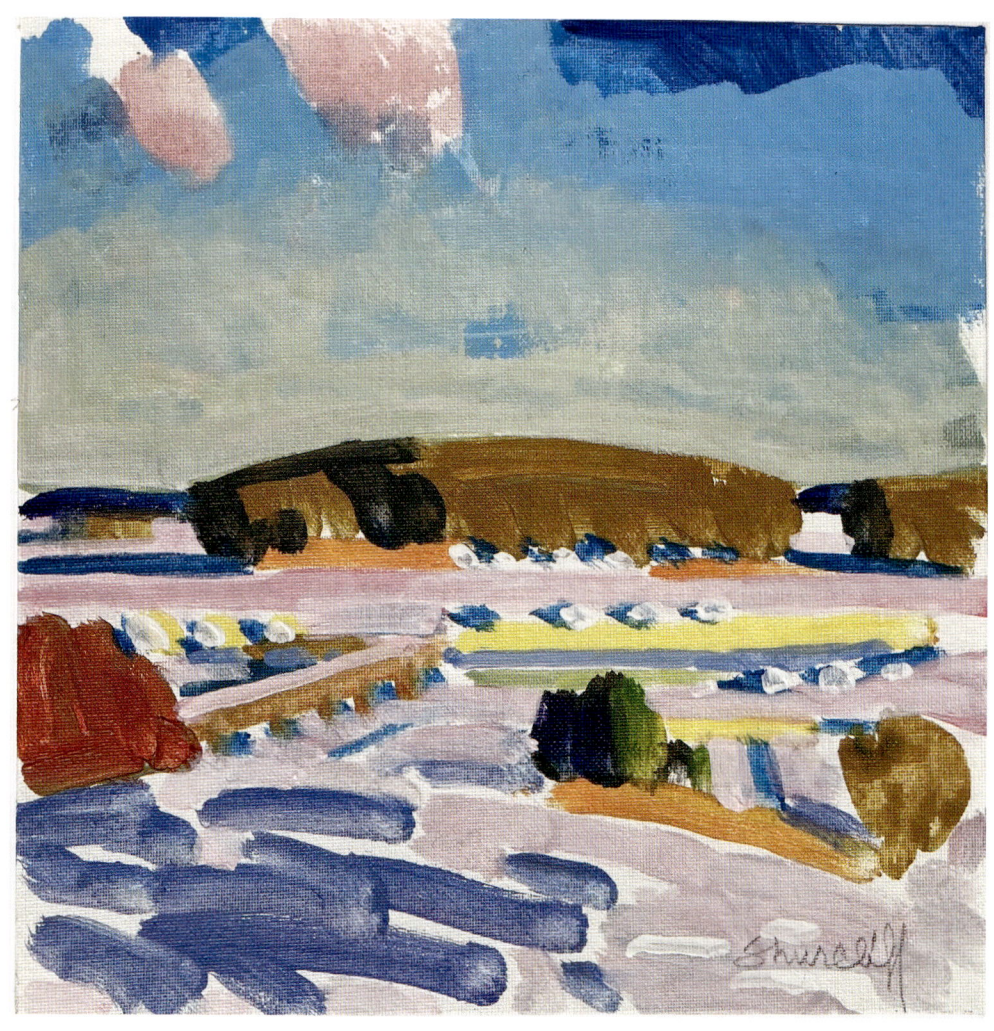

"The Great Marsh 42," acrylic on paper, Charles Shurcliff

looking, then directly applying the large color "passages" (swaths of color)
that correspond to structural forms creating the composition of the painting.
Cézanne was constantly adjusting and adding to the refinement of individual

hue relationships in a painting to create a powerful final resolution of cohesive color. We now know from medical MRIs that this technique of image comprehension models how our eyes and brain work naturally.

Color perspective is easiest to apply to the guesswork at the start of a painting in situ; for example, in a field or salt marsh. Layers of color that stretch out into the distance change with perceived depth from where you stand. The foreground is nearest to you, the middle-ground further into space, followed by the background furthest from your view. Your eye-level of the site where you are working is called the horizon. If you are sitting, it will be lower than if you stand. This line, most obvious at the edge of the sea, is the convergence of the sky and land (or water). It may be hidden by trees, distant hills, and other features, but you can determine its presence in your composition by using your viewfinder to decide how much land and sky will be in the image. You also can make a line estimating where the land vanishes up to meet the point where the sky vanishes down to the ground. The sky has the same three levels of depth to the horizon starting at the top of your page or canvas: again the foreground, middle-ground, and background. To create an illusion of depth for both the sky and land that meet at the horizon line, you will use the same color principles as those we exercise unconsciously in nature, such as color changing with perceived depth from where you stand to view the painting.

I like to describe color perspective in the way that I learned it from the writings of Emile Albert Gruppé, a Cape Ann landscape painter of the early twentieth century, who brought this theory to my attention and changed my view forever. It is helpful to imagine yourself outdoors with a friend who is standing next to you. Everything that you see in your immediate surroundings (the foreground) is local color. Your friend is wearing a red jacket that you see as a primary, bright, and saturated red. As he walks away from you into the distance, his jacket is the same, but its color begins to change with space between the two of you. If it is a clear, dry day, the color shift is subtle. On an overcast, humid day, the air loaded with water causes the color to become bluer and grayer as he moves closer to the horizon. This is the water-saturated air of a weather system that you used to make clothing choices or to plan a trek, which you can now use to predict color's placement in space. The more water, the more distortion of color that changes your friend's red jacket to a grayer, less vibrant, more purple shade as he moves further away into the distance. Details and contrast between elements also diminish with greater distance between you and drop from view. When you lose the ability to distinguish details and hue, all of your cones are firing at once, resulting in visual confusion—gray.

When I ask a new class to tell me a color that they think is one that lives in the background, someone always suggests black. I have come to understand that many have a visceral notion of color that is at a distance to them from their early understanding of color, which signals a hole in the ground or a deep cavity where light is absent. However, as a landscape painter, I seldom use black. Its appearance in a natural setting is startling and artificial. Most often there is too much light outdoors for black to exist. "Black is the absence of light." I've found that Mars Black paint mixed with Cadmium Yellow Light makes a wonderful deep green, though black used to adjust the color of pastels or most paint colors extinguishes the light in each color rather than darkening it for a desired value. Black's natural pigment form is rare, too, as is its optical presence in the furthest point of a field or marsh. Highly saturated black will create contrast, come forward, and push into the foreground in your illusion of space.

Blues, cool whites, and grays are the best choices for sitting at the edge of the horizon. The saturation of color—the amount of pure pigment or colors primary in nature and easily seen—exist in the foreground of both the land and sky. The purest, warmest, most vivid color of the field of grass should be placed at the bottom of your picture-plane. Conversely, the sky's blue should display the same characteristics of foreground color, the saturated blue at the top of the image can be more periwinkle or more green.

Warm colors, those that indicate sunlight or represent fire—red, orange, and yellow—are perceived as closer in space to us because of our affinity for warmth. These are colors that sit forward or jump into view. We naturally want to be warmed by their light in the landscape. In contrast, cooler colors appear to exist best out in the distance: the middle-ground and background. Water colors like teal greens and blue will remind us of the cooling properties of being wet, the wicking of heat from the surface of our skin as we swim and the chill of cold lakes, rivers, and the ocean. Snow and ice are the coldest sensations that we see in the landscape, so blue-whites and white recede into the distance due to our bodily aversion to cold elements.

The concept of using an optically mixed group of small paint passages, as perfected by George Seurat, of a primary color and its opposite, causes a vibrating effect that will appear to come forward within the picture-plane. This visual trick of using red, blue, or yellow with the corresponding opposite of green, orange, or purple will stimulate the viewer's cones to attention. White paint or pastel in the foreground or middle ground, like a patch of snow or the sand on a beach, will be changed optically by this same physiological response. It is called the Purple Cow theory. In a primarily yellow field, a white cow will offer a resting place for eyes that are overstimulated by the saturated color of the grasses. The highly light-reflective white form of the cow will appear purple, the release that your eyesight craves projected on the cow. See if you can imagine the color that a white cow will appear to be in an overwhelming sea of green grass? Your ability to estimate the color which will stimulate the foreground of the view means that you have color perspective as one of your tools to take with you as you head outside.

Value also predicts a color's placement in the landscape. The darkest dark is most often next to the lightest light, creating sharp contrast and coming forward. As color grays, or becomes less distinguished from the other colors in the vicinity due to the depth towards the horizon, muted relationships are indiscernible. Colors that blend together create the illusion of camouflage, another principle of color perspective that you already know and apply. Want to disappear in a crowd? Wear what everyone else is wearing.

The texture of the surface that reflects light can also change the color that you see and its value. As mentioned in the explanation of local color, a red jacket made of wool will gray and blue much sooner as it recedes into the distance. A shiny, reflective fabric or material will remain saturated even in the distance. These nuances help establish in elemental color the materials which make-up the scene that you are recreating in pastel or paint. Experiment with these few properties to establish a scale of relationships to express space and proportion out-of-doors and you will discover new visual tricks and color details of your own.

TRY THIS AT HOME OR ON THE TRAIL

Materials: a box of 6" x 9" Color-aid paper

Before you leave on a hike that will take you to an open view of a field or salt marsh, take the opportunity to imagine a green or yellow grassland under a cloudless sky using just color. Take out the color-applicable sheets of paper and arrange them (without tearing or cutting) in order of fore-ground, middle-ground, and background of the landscape. Then do the same thing, but starting at the top of the imagined picture plane for the sky down to the horizon. Try different colors that will create the illusion of space using the principles of color perspective explained above and push the limits of colors that could give you the most visual bang to bring your field of color into existence.

The more you repeat this exercise on the trail or at home, the more you will notice the color strategies that you have acquired using the concept of color perspective in the wild.

CHAPTER IV

COLORTROPISM

During the day, sunlight reflects from the surface of everything in view. A seedling penetrating the earth is warmed by the sun's rays and grows directly towards nature's universal energy source. Humans are moved by sunlight too. Our bodies respond to solar energy with all of our senses. We turn to warm ourselves instinctively, face drawn up into the blinding light for a moment to bask unshielded in the warm glow. Though we do

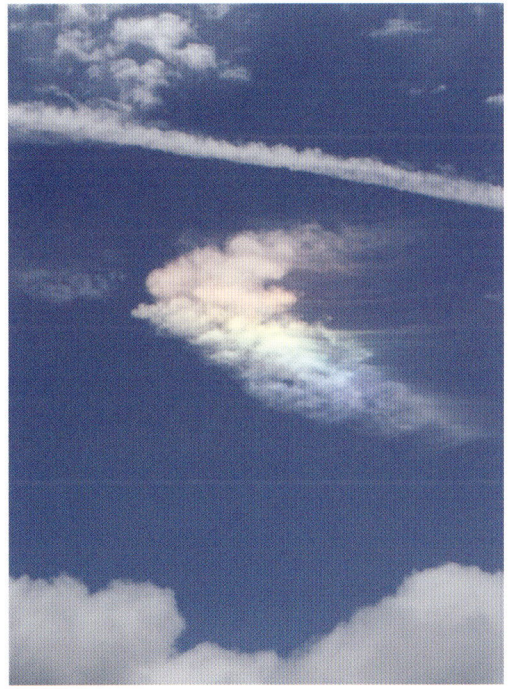

Photo, Colin Jermain

not photosynthesize like plants, we are heated, cooled, attracted, and repelled by sunlight's color.

I learned as a child to use the sun to counteract the darkness that distinguished my new home in New England from my birthplace in a sub-tropical climate. Forests dramatically shadowed the last leg of my family's cross-country drive to the Northeast, starting as we crossed the state line of New York. I was excited to see New England, unaware of the environmental eclipse that I would need to handle on my own. Our progressively more global world presents this same phototropic adjustment for the many who migrate today at a rate greater than at any other point in history. The need to adjust to the visual surroundings where you land is of critical importance to making a new habitat home.

Color control, which you will gain exploring hues' illusional properties in the landscape, will apply directly to the ideas that you might have for coloring the day-to-day habitat for you and your family. Your internal light meter can point the way to shades that satisfy your visual cravings. A hue can be optically hot or cold, reflecting the wavelength we see and absorbing all other light. Actual and perceived heat bounce off of a surface and persuade our senses to respond. The view of a warm red, surrounding our peripheral vision, raises our body temperature in a room without even registering on the thermostat. The reverse, cool blue walls in your office will drop your blood-pressure and quiet your mind in much the same way as a cold lake swim. Studies of children with Attention-Deficit/Hyperactivity Disorder (ADHD) reveal they experience calm in a sunlit yellow space, suggesting that color can elicit behavior on par with a stimulant drug like Ritalin.

Color becomes a powerful tool when you recognize the human behavior it elicits. Long held, multi-sensory memories of what we've found in nature are triggered repeatedly by hue. Our visual understanding of the world of our childhood comes from careful inspection—first seeing and assessing, then studying more closely with our touch, smell, taste, and even hearing. This practice has filled our memory bank with examples of what we have seen and discerned. A color can cause us to wince as if it were sour, repulsed from its putrid tone. The commercial names of colors (i.e., Sour Apple, Mozart Blue, Frosted Rose, Dill Pickle—Benjamin Moore Paints) demonstrate that we ascribe taste, sound, touch, and smell to express our responses to and distinguish versions of each wavelength of sunlight that form the colors of a rainbow.

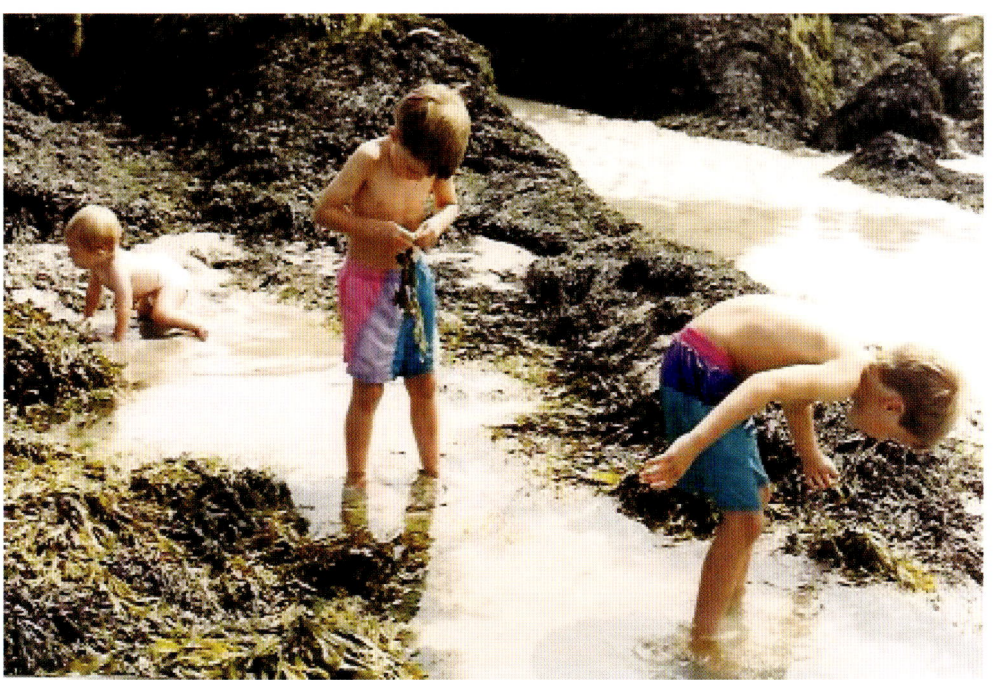

Color study, Coffins Beach, Gloucester, MA

The latitude on the globe where we formed our earliest awareness, the intensity of the light there each day, and seasonally, has colored our memory with what to expect from what we see. Our ancestors' optical traits, which we have inherited genetically from their physical adaptations to the intensity of the sun, can influence our response to color. North of the arctic circle, nations of peoples with light irises are highly sensitive to subtle shifts in color. Individuals with dark irises respond best to color that is higher in chromatic value and a bigger color punch of sunlight. While sharing in a class the exercise in Chapter I that focuses attention on one's reflexive response to a saturated primary, one brown-eyed student was having trouble seeing the afterimage that all others in the class could report. I took the exercise outside and had the student focus on the sample of color in full sunlight. This student of African ancestry easily projected an afterimage on the glowing white backdrop outdoors, though it had eluded her indoors.

Artists, architects, and designers who wish to more specifically tailor their work to stimulate the personal visual consciousness of a client or user group must consider the environment where the work will be displayed or inhabited, as well as the global origins of the users. Nuances in color adaptation and preferences can be unique to both individuals and cultural groups as a whole. These nuances can also reflect age differences and, as mentioned earlier in this field guide, gender strengths and weaknesses.

Sunlight is at the heart of color preferences that will condition our lives. A library requires a quiet mood that can be created by a dark tone, warm or cool. But a family's playroom would not inspire fun if gray hung over the space like a storm cloud. Once a color is selected that meets the activity needs of the use of the space, the value can be adjusted, darker or lighter, to aid in bouncing light from the walls further into the room. Don't forget that the floor is a great opportunity to carry light into the interior and energize it with color. The ceiling, as well, provides a surface to reflect light from windows and artificial sources to where it is needed within the layout. In extremely dark rooms destined to be used during the day, designers often make the most of available light by incorporating mirrors, shiny surfaces, and large landscape paintings or other luminous art.

In architecture and design, listening to the language that a client uses to describe their objectives and personal preferences provides clues to the thermal expectations of an individual. Knowing a client intuitively likes the idea of "dill pickle" tells me that they crave a saltiness to the design that we are discussing. One woman rejected "the perfect color" (her words, not mine) sampled on-site because of the name, which didn't appeal. Color preferences can be fickle. It also underscores the need to suss out the root of another person's color ideas and make sure language is precise. When someone I am working with asks for a palette that is "crisp," I know that they are referring to contrast, maybe a detail of white trim standing forward or a dark accent color. I am careful to use common color words followed by paper color samples. But clients are not expected to be precise or even mean what they say. One time, a palette of subtle browns formed the color plan for an individual who said from the outset that they wanted me to know that they do not like brown. Yet while on-site sampling color, they were consistently selecting brown. As the owner's understanding and vision changed through the process, she realized how color worked in her own home, unlike the brown couch color her mother had insisted upon for their childhood TV room to camouflage dirt.

Color associations are difficult to work around or even explore because they are personal and can be emotional. The best collaborative process lets each individual share their color intuition and try out each other's ideas on-site. The more closely your color meter relates to reality, the more you can trust this important give-and-take in the process.

Sunsations

Warm, saturated colors are energized by the sun's radiant hot plasma that we orbit each day. We are naturally drawn to the heat. Our blood pressure will rise in a positive way when we are in a room with walls that reflect a fire's red glow. In a terra-cotta-colored dining room, spirits are high, cued by the atmosphere of colors stimulating appetite and conviviality. Simply surrounding a person's peripheral vision with a color that has an element of the warm light of the sun will improve one's mood like a clear summer day.

The reverse is also true; the muted colors of dormancy, such as the grays of winter storms, remind us of the prolonged, deep sleep induced by cold, known as hibernation. Paint a room with the gray of cloud cover and you will replicate the quieting effect and rest inspired by a rainy day. In a bedroom, this may be what induces the sleep you long for. Overall, knowing how you respond to color that is visceral can help you make choices that will support your circadian rhythm and regulate your sleep-wake cycle naturally with light.

Some individuals who are particularly responsive to the amount of sunshine they experience each day may require taking added steps to address what is known as Seasonal Affective Disorder (SAD). This medical condition points out an individual's unique sensitivity to daily light requirements or the lack thereof, which triggers depression. To ameliorate the condition, someone who studies color can bring to bear a highly responsive internal light meter and intuit the needs of others by shaping the design for maximum comfort, whether it is for a living or work space. Many people often miss such solutions because they have not done what you are doing with *Nature of Color*: getting outside to explore in-depth how the sun's wavelengths create color and mood.

The system that paint companies and manufacturers use to determine a color's light reflecting capacity is called the LRV—Light Reflective Value—which measures the visible light that radiates from the surface of paint or other materials. The LRV varies with hue and value. Lighter colors, such as white or light yellow, are highly reflective and have the highest value. Colors with a high LRV can be counted on to bring sunlight across the surface of a wall or floor to where you may need it deeper into the space. Conversely, black, dark blues, and dark greens that absorb light have low LRV values. Low LRV colors dampen the light of a space, softening reflection and retaining heat on the surface. Outdoors, a dark color with a low LRV in full sun can cause some materials to heat up and break down.

It is critical to consider the heat that is associated with a low LRV color when applying paint or considering a man-made product that could melt in the midday sun. Those who test color on-site regularly are continually improving their own internal light meters for evaluating reflectivity. However, for commercial products that must stay within an LRV range to be compliant with a warranty, using the LRV metric is simple to assess conditions and avoid problems.

Create a Sundial

Materials: four 2" oval rocks, eight pea-stone-sized rocks, one straight 12" stick, a compass

You already know the rooms in your home that you enjoy at different times of the day for sunlight and warmth. The site of your house has seasonal advantages and disadvantages too. The structure itself will invariably block light that might be advantageous for your floor plan and your family's use of the space. A landscape of evergreen trees might do the same. Creating a sundial outside in a shadowless, level clearing is the best way to show the relationship of your home to the movement of the sun from first light of the morning, to where activities are best midday, to the leisure hours of the evening.

First, locate north on your phone's compass. Place one of the oval rocks at the top of an imagined compass face pointing north. Place a second oval rock directly opposite in the position south, with a compass diameter of about 18 inches from north to south. Next, place the remaining oval rocks to correspond to the cardinal compass positions of east and west. Fill in from north to east with a pea-stone rock to correspond to one and two on the clock dial, then four and five, seven and eight, and ten and eleven, completing the clock face of stones. Now push the straight stick into the ground in the middle of the circle of stones. The stick's shadow should point to the time as a single hour hand would. Check the accuracy of your sundial with an analog watch. If the dial is off, reposition the stones using your compass until the time is correct.

Find other ways to observe the movement of light in your home and the use of those who live there. I enjoy watching how my cat moves through the house, finding warmth in the morning sun of the bright kitchen and then moving to the shaded entry alcove for coolness in the hot afternoon. Despite some pets having limited color vision, it is instructive to watch their movements in response to sunlight's heat. They remind us to watch how light changes our spaces over the day and over the seasons. In cooler months, they are attracted to the heated rays of sunlight brought in through windows and providing a warm, sunny space to relax and enjoy. During the heat of summer, they seek shade under beds and in the north rooms of the house. If the upholstered chair needs to be "de-furred" regularly, this is a pet-approved site for reading and repose that you both can enjoy.

TRY THIS ON THE BEACH OR TRAIL

Materials: one straight 12" stick

Follow the same process above, inscribing the sundial in the sand or dirt.

My father taught our family to use sundials at the beach to tell time wherever we roamed since we didn't wear watches in the summer. The direction of magnetic north was pointed out to us then checked with our father's watch. We learned to quickly make a clock face in the sand with a stick, forming a dial with carefully positioned points for the four cardinal directions of the compass rose from memory. Sometimes a slightly skewed face could be checked by the state of the tide, adjusted to get closer to what we intuitively thought was the actual time. When we were late for something that mattered to us, it taught us to be more accurate with making the dial the next time around.

Keeping our daily schedule with an awareness of the sun and moon's movements in relation to where we inhabit the earth indelibly influences your perception of time and space in a three-dimensional way.

Colordial

TRY THIS AT HOME

At home, collect a rainbow of single-color items (primary and secondary colors are best) and place them following the inside arch of the sundial that you have created where you feel the warm or cool colors relate best to their distance from the sun. The northern orientation of the circle should represent cooler blue light; the southern side, the warmer colors that light up the mid-day.

TRY THIS ON THE TRAIL

Materials: colored paper, pastels or paints or natural colored materials

On the trail, use color paper samples, colored pastels or paints that you have brought on your hike, or collect natural materials such as shells, berries, rocks, and wood (always be careful to leave poisonous plants out of the design). To replicate the rainbow of color resembling a color wheel, place color choices evenly spaced around the face of the sundial. Starting at north, order blue, purple, red, orange, yellow, and green. This exercise will lead you to a perspective on the range of color in the environment that you are exploring and will refine what you can now enjoy as your inner "colortropism" meter for estimating color's power and influence.

TRY THIS AT HOME AND ON THE TRAIL

Materials: sand (or similar material) of varying hues

Navajo sand paintings, also known as dry paintings, have been created for centuries on the dirt floor of the family hogan (the traditional home) to offer the gods a place to interact with earth and intercede in issues of health and harvest. Created by dropping a stream of colored sand onto the ground, figures are formed within a circular picture frame compatible with the radius of the interior space within the shelter. The figuration and circular layout of the mythology reflects indigenous people's spiritual and day-to-day perception of their relationship with the earth's natural cycles and their respect for the powerful forces of the lunar and solar systems that guide their lives.

By creating a "colordial" within the circle of your sundial, you will be orienting yourself to the solar color system for retaining a memory of the important relationship between light and hue. With a little pre-planning, this exercise can be explored outside at home or on the trail. The model that you create to track the sun's path will mirror the colors reflected throughout the day. Outside your home, you will see the influence of the landscape, geography, and built environment and predict what can be experienced indoors as a result of your window plan. On the trail, your explorations with sun and color dials will illustrate the macro level of awareness that can be gained by keeping the sun's path in mind for navigation and estimating the progress of your trek.

Learned Sensations

Color is an attention-getter the world over. Our whole body can be halted abruptly by signage that is simply bright red. Caution tape is sunshine yellow to trigger the same response, and most people will make sure to avoid the color-marked area without a word of instruction. International orange on a lifejacket makes the wearer visible to others out at sea. On upholstery, orange grabs attention towards the seating area of a public place to lounge with others in a school or library. Color's powerful but silent voice is one that can be put into action to help a product stand out from the many others on the shelf or communicate ideas in a design directly.

Learning the cultural cues that can be employed to reach out and hold attention starts with taking a look at perceptual traditions that have been passed down through history. In western cultures and contemporary Asia, where reading is from left to right, you can expect those entering a public entry space to naturally move to the left while circulating to the right as they look for visual cues to point the way. In contrast, traditional written Chinese is read from top to bottom, with ancient custom favoring a vertical format of anticipated visual signage to provide clues. Using color as a universal language, culturally sensitive designers can employ a strategically placed hue, or a series of related colors, to signal visitors that they are on the right track in an unfolding space.

Our cultural experience informs what looks right where color is concerned. Holidays celebrated around the globe use the stimulating effects of a primary with an opposite. For example, Christmas's red and green or Easter's purple and yellow. We know from physiology that the pairing of opposites, also known as complementary colors, engages all color receptors simultaneously with a stimulating vibrating effect that adds excitement to the festivities. The same strategy is used for sports teams and school colors. The European tradition of white for celebrating weddings and black expressing sorrow at a funeral is in contrast to Asia's use of white for funerals and red for weddings. The simple gesture of wearing the appropriate color expresses your feelings of happiness or loss.

Unconsciously, we make quick assumptions about situations from the color code we've learned, along with acquiring our verbal language. Intuitive color speculations can influence our linear thinking about color that may not reflect the facts. An example of this is the common acceptance of historical color palettes available from many commercial and residential paint companies. In an effort to restore historic properties with color that "matched" samples taken from the surfaces of exceptional properties, a grayed palette of colors was formulated to be used with particular styles representing historical periods of architecture. More recent paint analysis has determined that colors presented as "historic" did not account for the aging of the paint that caused the colors to be grayer and more muted than the original application specified by the architect. It is important to recognize that our first color impulses have merit but must be considered within the context of the color objectives that we set out. What you know in depth about the situation that requires a color plan should guide use, especially for costly installations.

Working with thousands of individuals expressing their views about color, I have come to believe that like sugar, hue has the ability to heighten our senses for excitement and increase our tolerance for more and more saturation. Subtle colors can be dismissed as being "without color" by those who crave more impact. Light-sensitive people prefer the quiet of natural pigments and may object to saturated samples of stronger pigments, calling them "loud" without seeing the perspective where the color will sit in context. Sampling a color in the primer stage gives everyone involved the benefit of "seeing" for themselves in actual size and relationship to assess the dimensional impact and avoid living with color that misses the mark due to presumptions out of step with reality.

The French painter Eugène Delacroix, considered one of the last of the European Old Masters, decided for an 1830s trip to Spain and Algiers in North Africa that he would experiment in the sun-drenched light of the equator with newly produced paints of high saturation. His paintings, when exhibited upon his return to Paris, influenced the Impressionists and then other schools of painters who sought the optical effects illuminated by the new palette. Delacroix's lively brushstrokes, figures in motion, and high chromatic reds and Naples yellow distinguished his work from the browner palettes of other salon painters of the time. By inspiring a significant palette shift, he is thought to have ushered in the modern era of painting.

In architecture and the arts, the combination of new technology and the vision of contemporary practitioners propel swings in fashion. These swings not only set style, but also change the taste cravings for hue that sway the public's interest in color to light up their lives.

CHAPTER V

FORAGE

Humans are visually challenged each day to navigate, explore, and witness the environment. Man-made structures of the urban setting provide a square and plumb frame through which to observe other people, their pets, their material possessions, and their debris. Even in the city, nature's color influences how we perceive public spaces with atmospheric hues of sunlight and clouds highlighting the buildings and streetscapes.

Just beyond the city limits, man's influence starts to drop away and nature has the upper hand. Unpredictable open terrain, beating to its own playlist of sights, sounds, and smells, forms a laboratory for me where I find my senses become activated; awareness, sharpened. Immediately, a large exhale begins the rhythm of my movements foraging for color. It is my sacred routine to acquaint myself and connect with Mother Nature. My creative practice depends on it. Each time I head to the natural world for study or relaxation, I add to my empirical store of examples of how color works to deliver new sensations that appeal to all of my senses.

The extemporary method of color study that you have perfected over your life-time is an evolutionary adaptation that has worked for you and for those whom your art and design can reach and dazzle. To access your personal "hard drive" of color memory, add to your discipline a tradition to forage for color with new intent. On a more ritualized hunt to find color, you engage on a new level with the universal resource for light, color, and life: the sun. This nod to being part of a larger world may make it easier for various audiences to identify with your resulting visual creations.

A few years ago, I opened an Instagram account for the purpose of sharing photos of Found Color from my walks in nature. I wanted to take advantage of the technology I carried along with me most of the time to share color finds that excited my interest. I was also developing a curriculum for middle school students to raise their heads up from their phones and actually use the device to learn about finding color in their environment. Though I seldom feel the need to chronicle my own life in snapshots, I know others communicate daily this way. I wanted to see for myself if what I was finding outdoors might be of interest to my family and friends.

After a year of Instagram images, Found Color became a thing. Friends started to post their own examples from wherever they happened to be at a moment when color stopped them in their tracks. I was similarly moved by their posts with an unconscious gasp inhaled at the sight of amazing color framed by our phones. I was taken to places I'd never been, on walks that I had missed. Making pictures and sharing them with your social media audience, and vice versa, can generate a color data culture over time so that your colorful ideas can hit the spot with visual relevance.

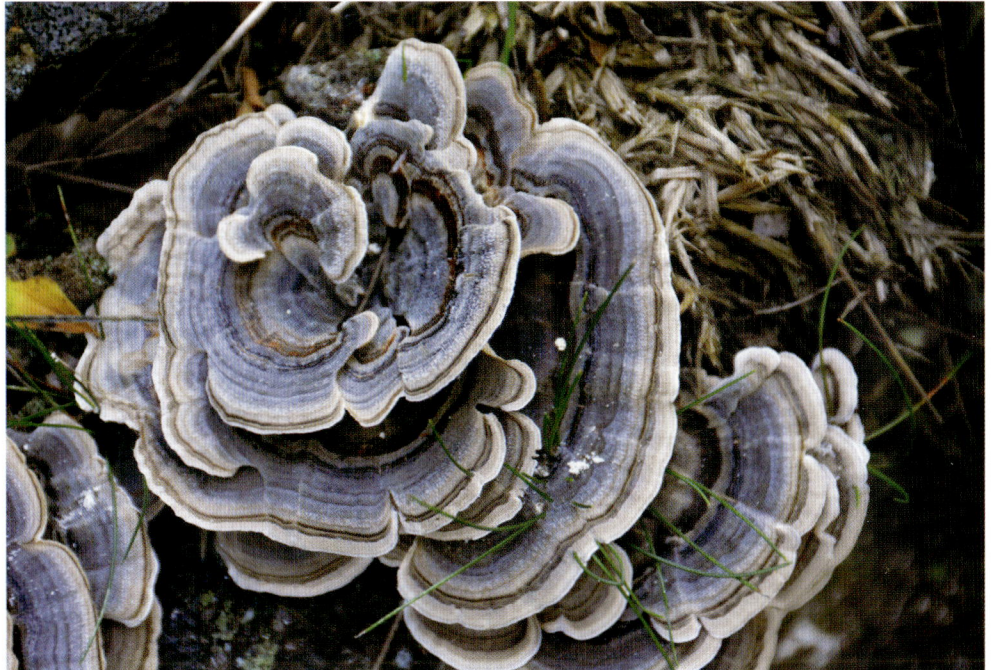

"Turkey Tails," Mike Dyer

Caching

If you decide to take on the challenge of foraging regularly in nature, you will not be the only one scavenging for eye-appealing colors. A bee's color vision is trichromatic like our own, meaning their retinas have cone cells that detect three primary colors. However, the receptors of bees differ from our own. The three colors of light that human cones are sensitive to are red, blue, and green— our brains do the blending to perceive periwinkle blue, sienna brown, and all other hues in our visual world. On the other hand, bees see yellow, blue, and ultraviolet most easily. Other winged creatures adding to the air-traffic outdoors are birds well-known for their discerning color perception. Not only do birds have a high number of receptors to aid their forage on the fly, their visual acuity is sensitive to ultraviolet light, just like bees. Is this a "chicken or egg" example of what came first? Can increasing our color vision practice improve our scavenging techniques and our visual acuity to match that of the birds and bees? I believe so!

A curious thing happens when passion infuses our relationship with a subject of our fascination. The desire to wrap our arms around something, with everything we have in our sensory toolkit, can transport us across unconscious barriers. Children easily display unbridled joy exploring their curiosity in this way.

I had the happy task of rowing my children to and from their nursery school. One morning as my youngest son arrived and hung his lifejacket up on his coat hook, he turned and announced that he was going to "taste everything at the bottom of the sea." This was met with a resounding "YUCK" by the classroom of children. It was painful to watch Nate's exuberance quickly turn to shame. Thankfully, his explorations of the marine world were unstoppable. A few days later, as he handled the fish in the live-well that was used to keep bait fresh on his father's boat and served as an aquarium for the boys, I noticed Nate chewing something. I asked what was in his mouth, and he lifted his head and said that he was chewing "gum." His favorite book at the time was about an Alaskan boy who fished with his family. Inuit children take the lens out of the codfish's eye and chew the rubber-like material for gum. Nate even today gets to know a fishery by testing and tasting.

There are many ways to stimulate your brain to focus on a subject that you are studying. Drawing or painting the colors you witness in nature is a fundamental method to encourage keen observation. The act of committing your color choices to paper, and adapting them to read in relation to each other, makes the color experience memorable and allows you to replicate what you see more convincingly. You can increase even further the receptivity of your brain to outdoor visual stimulus by adding body movement, such as posing, stretching, or swimming.

Synesthesia is described as a condition experienced by those who associate one sensory input with the added sensation of another unstimulated sense. The example often given, the one I could relate to as a child, was visualizing numbers and letters in color. For me, color brought the dull construct of the black-and-white written words and numbers that I was learning in school into my full-color visual world. Sounds and smells are often used to trigger memories of visual sights, which are more vivid with the added sensory prompts. Nate was using synesthesia to explore his passion for fish, naturally.

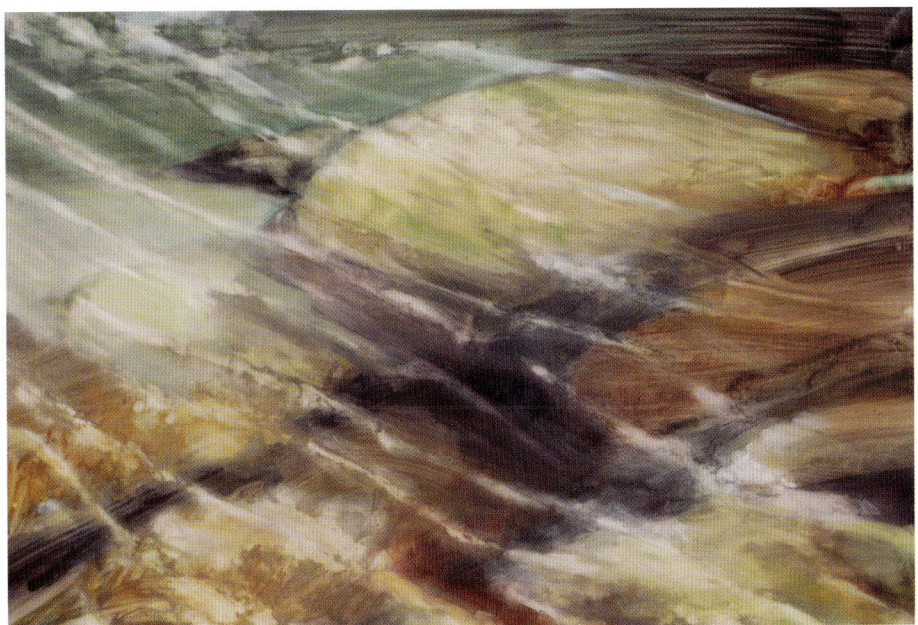

"Summer Shallows," oil on panel, White Beach, Manchester, MA

I don't think synesthesia is an unusual "condition." I view it as a powerful tool to develop the neuropathways in the brain to heighten visual perception and recall. Just as movement on a hike may enhance your observations of color, so will engaging all your senses help to retain the visual information that you have before you. For example, to help retrieve the impressive natural color effects I observe while snorkeling underwater, I chew edible seaweed back in my studio. First, while in the water, I draw the color coming into my consciousness. My method there in the cool water-filled quarry or along the shoreline of the North Atlantic is to use oil sticks on recycled plastic YUPO paper taped to a plastic cutting board. Back at the studio, munching on bits of edible seaweed, my olfactory receptors are stimulated by the release of smells similar to the seaweed that I swam around in the intertidal zone. This synesthesia helps me recreate the exhilarating color discovered during my day's swim.

TRY THIS ON THE TRAIL

Materials: *Nature of Color*, 24 box set of Prismacolor pastels, Pop Rocks edible candy

Do this exercise in an aquatic setting in a fresh or saltwater marsh or any place plants need air bladders to float up towards sunlight. One place might be where rock weed grows like fringe, dressing the rocks revealed at low tide.

The popular candy Pop Rocks is made of sugar using high-pressure CO_2. When the grains of sugar pieces hit the heated moisture of your mouth, they explode with a crackling sensation of sound and air escaping against the inside of your mouth. After exploring the rock weed bed or marsh area on foot, settle yourself onto a dry area in a posture that will allow you to look at and draw a segment of the colors of seaweed that you see. Open your mouth and drop the Pop Rocks onto your tongue. Now take your box of pastels and paint what you see in the intertidal area or aquatic environment. This quick color study should be a detail of the vegetation that you observe rather than a grand view of the landscape. Notice how your choices respond to the Pop Rocks, reinforcing the texture and character of the rock weed you are studying in color.

CAUTION: If you are at the coastline, be sure to keep an eye on the tide.

TRY THIS AT HOME

Materials: *Nature of Color*, 24 box set of Prismacolor pastels, edible seaweed

A few weeks after your hike along the coastline or aquatic habitat, use a page in your field guide or a separate piece of paper to draw what you remember from the experience of studying vegetation. While you work, chew a small piece of seaweed or the root of a cat tail to create the environment again through taste and smell. (If you enjoy the Pop Rocks, here's your excuse to indulge once again!)

As you move forward with your explorations, come up with your own tricks to generate sensations that will support memories of the color you find outside: a scented oil diffuser, a bowl of acorns or Eucalyptus seed pods, a nature sounds playlist, or gifts of nature scavenged along the way.

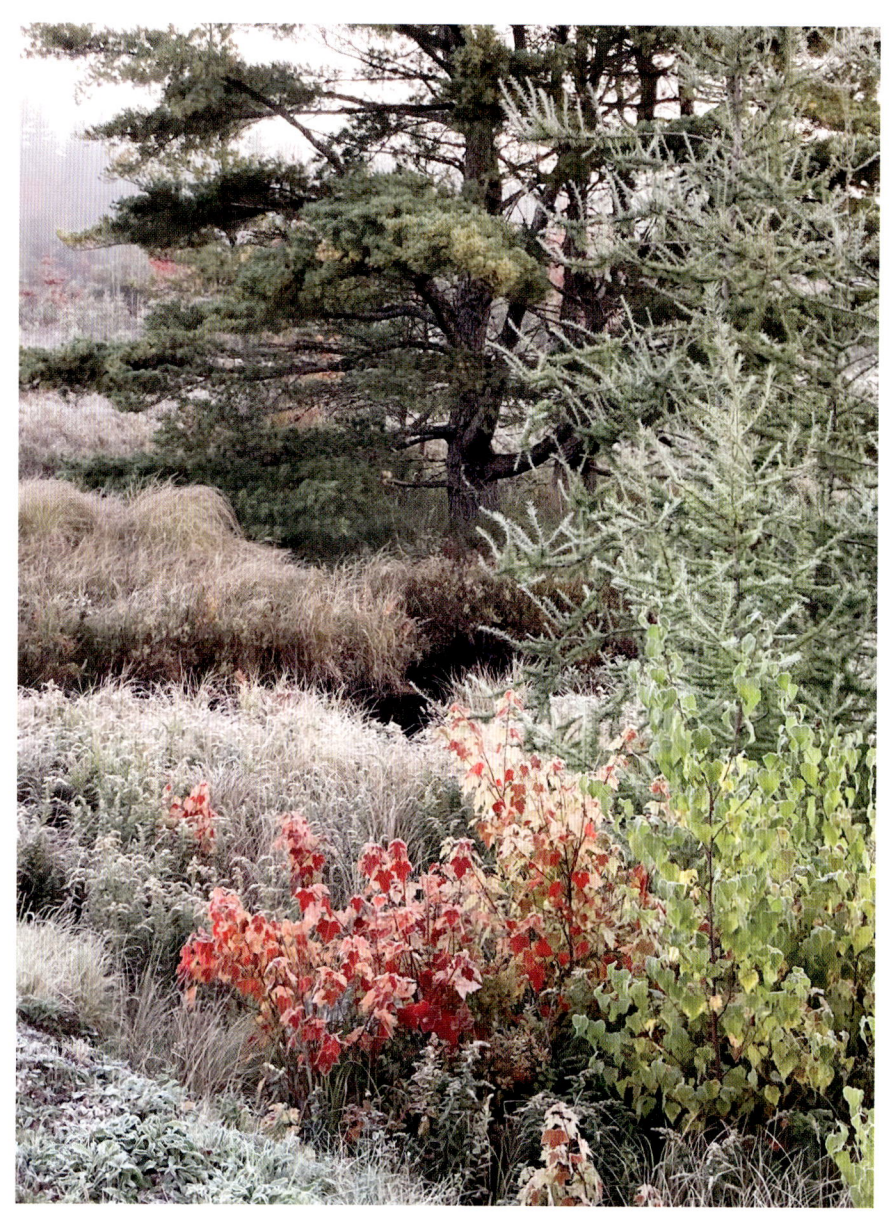

Morning frost, Nova Scotia, Canada

Collecting Color

It is difficult for me to return from a walk on the beach without dragging something home that appeared to have been left on my path divinely. The shoreline is the shoot end of a masterful recycling system. Physical transformations of flotsam and jetsam are tumbled for weeks, months, even years in the wave action of the marine environment. These refinished finds are then deposited on the beach for the scavenger. I marvel at my good timing when my hand clutches a beautiful shell.

As a young specimen collector, I was often overly discriminating. Each time I left behind a rejected shell or sand dollar, realizing too late its value to the collection back at home, my reverse trip to retrieve it rarely worked out. Most often the tide had taken it back. I learned that it was better to keep an open mind and leave the editing for a few days. Otherwise, I found that I missed something which had caught my eye for a reason. There is nothing like regret to focus vision on the next beach trek—and few things in life are guaranteed like the ocean's return policy for accepting a treasure that gets re-evaluated.

My family's beach house was a temporary depository for our favorite ocean detritus. It provided clues for what was going on all around us and, most importantly, a window into the depths of the powerful ocean that we looked upon in awe. My parents only casually tried to stem the tide of beach bric-a-brac that showed up in my bedroom. Their gentle acceptance was admirable and prevented my mother from appearing sanctimonious, given her large personal collection on the window ledges and the giant driftwood tree that she convinced a backhoe driver to bring up from the beach to the front of the house. My younger sister's boxes of dead birds under the bed were annoying, but clearly fueled her vast knowledge of ornithology. My little brother was allowed to keep his catch, the full body of a small bluefish, in the freezer to revisit and study. Countless times the specimen softened under his hot little hands and warm breath and had to be put away for future sessions of inspection.

With your own beach combing, have you ever noticed how the color of natural specimens found on a beach become dull and lifeless when retrieved from your pockets? It can be hard to see why you picked them up in the first place from the field of thousands littering the sand. For beach foundlings especially, water is needed to revive the color that first caused you to extend your grasp under-water where they appeared larger, more brilliant, magnified by the watery lens. Then, as years pass and your collection grows as a pile on the window ledge or side table, the color returns because the specimens are visible in context to one another. The wow that moved you to select them may be a fading sensation, but now the treasures seen juxtaposed to one another can evoke color memory. As the collection grows as a whole, it renders in miniature the dynamics of color play, depth, and perspective.

Sometimes the memory of a colorful Found Object is more electrifying than the real thing. I'm compelled to paint the experience of what first caught my eye in nature's context, which is softer, more subtle, and silent. In the studio, white walls restore the color and detail to the specimen by contrasting it to the highly reflective light of the space. But nature is not a museum or a studio; the contrast that allows the color to pop once again tells a different story than the one that I gathered up with my prize. I opt to relay the color story found at its natural source that is exquisite on its own terms. To do so, I paint color in its context, versus color taken out of context and contrasted by artificial studio lights, bright canvas, or paper. Training my mind to retain context helps me to paint color that is stunning and authentic. It requires using every perceptual imprinting technique that I know of.

What follows are some ways you can stretch the color creativity that is unique to your discoveries. By connecting the dots yourself rather than following specific instructions, you can better remember the original view when you make it visible again in paint.

Colorful Language

In middle school, children explore language and are warned to keep it clean. The reason given to me to avoid using swear words—"It's a sign of someone with a poor vocabulary"—didn't jibe with the multitude of words that seemed to offer descriptions of things my friends and I really wanted to know more about for conversations on the phone. Colorful language was precisely what we were interested in adding to our vocabulary.

At the same time that I had my ears peeled for racy new words, I learned to use metaphor from a friend and classmate who liberally applied this device in conversation, giving us a direct flight into her imagination. I was awestruck by the simplicity of the act that retooled my own perceptions to align with hers. I practiced using analogies at the family dinner table and found that the best examples brought the description to life for everyone, including me, and they stuck. Metaphor is the work of the artist. I know now, Andrea was flexing her artist's muscles as she tested out her audience's capabilities to follow along. I borrowed her example and found the courage to use the method for making metaphors to fit my own designs.

TRY THIS AT HOME AND ON THE TRAIL

Materials: *Nature of Color*

Color will easily refine your observations and embellish your stories. Keep a log of colorful language in your field guide as your vocabulary increases with descriptors and expressions. Try your hand at metaphors and start using them in your conversations on the trail. You will be creating a glossary of terms to enhance your communications, both with auditory and visual dimensions. Your color word collections can be illustrated with paper samples or left to the imagination.

The "double entendre" can be fun to invent and collect; leave it to the French to spice up our lives with unforgettable ways to enjoy the risqué. Even the Benjamin Moore Paints "Index of Color" is filled with color names that can inspire and push the envelope of your imagination. Colors such as Bridal Pink, Bleeker Beige, Mighty Aphrodite, Inner Peach, and Broken Arrow add intrigue—and also reveal the difficulty of coming up with thousands of color names for a single brand of paint!

Color Field

Large expanses of color vibrate with energy and excite my personal interest in painting landscapes. Once I got over my disappointment in modern art history that the Color Field Painters were not painting fallow landscapes in sunlight, I forgave the brashness of artists like Jackson Pollock, Kenneth Nolan, Morris Lewis, Helen Frankenthaler, Mark Rothko, and others who used color athletically to excite their audience. After all, their approach to color was admirable, if unorthodox.

By and large, the mid-twentieth century art focused on the artists' audacity to change the rules with the medium of paint. The Color Field Painters took the energy of Expressionism, the work of Willem de Kooning and Franz Kline, on center stage and blew it up into landscape scale. Size alone shifted the view, dropping away the figurative, such as the human body or nature, for now the subject was the medium's own whims. Color alone spoke for these painters as they showed off their daring. Installations of their work in the quiet of a gallery could shake your sense of equilibrium. This full-on effect was the goal of the Color Field Painters as they offered the viewer, unknowingly for many, a color theory code to unlock the displays. That frustrated some and enthralled others. I was on the enthralled spectrum, but as a young painter, I did not fit the macho personality that was required to keep the public guessing and engaged. But the intensity of the color in their works could be felt standing a few feet away, and I wanted to have that skill in my tool box. I looked to science to clue me in.

As I trained to become a painter, I found myself between the realist painters who taught me to see critically and craft an image and those artists who sought to "throw it all away and start over" in their search of a gimmick that would entertain the public and carry the artist to stardom. Science was the place where I found a correction, clear understandings, and an underpinning to teach what was inexplicable. I was lucky to be influenced by the Bauhaus expats who had fled Germany and were then living in towns like my own west of Boston. Their pre-WWII school began in Europe, an intersection between art and design crafts. Later in New England, their indelible influence was woven into the arts culture everywhere I turned. Growing up in this milieu, I came up with a life plan to make the best out of a creative life taught to me by Mother Nature: an entrepreneurial mash-up for continuing as a painter while also teaching and working as an architectural color designer, using my skills in color illusion.

In recent years, and particularly in times of economic downturns, entrepreneurial spirit is touted as the way to drive innovation, produce unique products, and create jobs. My family's experience living at the beach each summer—one that was isolated from the rest of the city where we lived—taught us to use nature to our advantage. We learned to anticipate nature's opportunities and gain marketable skills; in short, be entrepreneurial. There would not be a car available to get to a job outside the beach area, so we five siblings created work where we were: serving as party boat captain, providing launch service, teaching nature programs, running a house painting crew, lifeguarding, and private coaching for swimming and sailing. As an adult, I have taken my family's enterprising spirit into my work life and career. It influences my entire approach to using color.

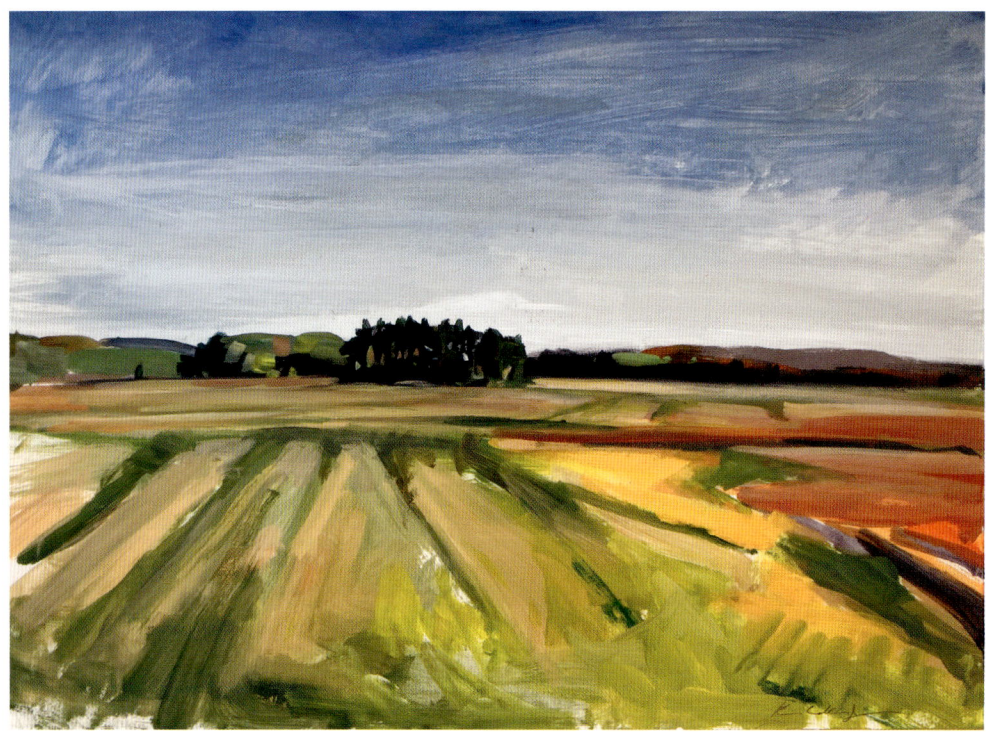

"Charlie's Side of the Marsh," acrylic on paper, Ipswich, MA

TRY THIS AT HOME AND ON THE TRAIL

Materials: *Nature of Color*

Memory is such an important part of vision that tracing your own significant influences can tell you how you see. Use the journal pages in *Nature of Color* to record some of the color events or past geography in your life that still resonate in your foraging for color where you live now or where you travel. Keep a running list or write a blog as a color-journalist. This activity guides artists in their reflection and the development of content, from the art itself to the artist's statement.

TRY THIS AT HOME

Materials: Color-aid paper or colored construction paper

This is an exercise I do with a group of students at the start of a class to get to know how they see and what they are thinking about. It is simple and will help you review the theory of "color perspective" so that you understand it before going out onto the trail.

Take three colors from your color-aid or construction paper palette, any color at all. Now lay them down in front of you on a table and hold them in a landscape, horizontal direction. Now organize them in how they would appear in space from foreground, middle-ground, or background. Make your best solution to the exercise. There is some subjectivity to the choices, but try out a couple of the arrangements to see what is visually effective and note why that is.

Color Field Painting

Materials: *Nature of Color*, Color-aid paper, glue stick

I prefer to do this exercise outdoors, but that is not always possible with weather and time. If you must perform it indoors, project a simple photograph of an empty field or marsh onto a screen. If you are outside, first define the image through your viewfinder and take a picture with your phone for a record. Next, identify the horizon line of the landscape. Locate the foreground, middle-ground, and background of both the ground and sky. Now use torn paper to create a color study of the landscape, gluing the pieces down after you have had a chance to try them out in a dry mock-up of your color choices. Make sure you get up every twenty minutes to walk around and clear your vision, both inside and outside. Post the finished piece on your kitchen refrigerator, like Matisse would do. The results from my students are so beautiful that despite the difficulty at first, this is one of the best opportunities I've found for them to learn color perspective. I hope you will be inspired to do this collaging exercise often to take your color vision to the next level.

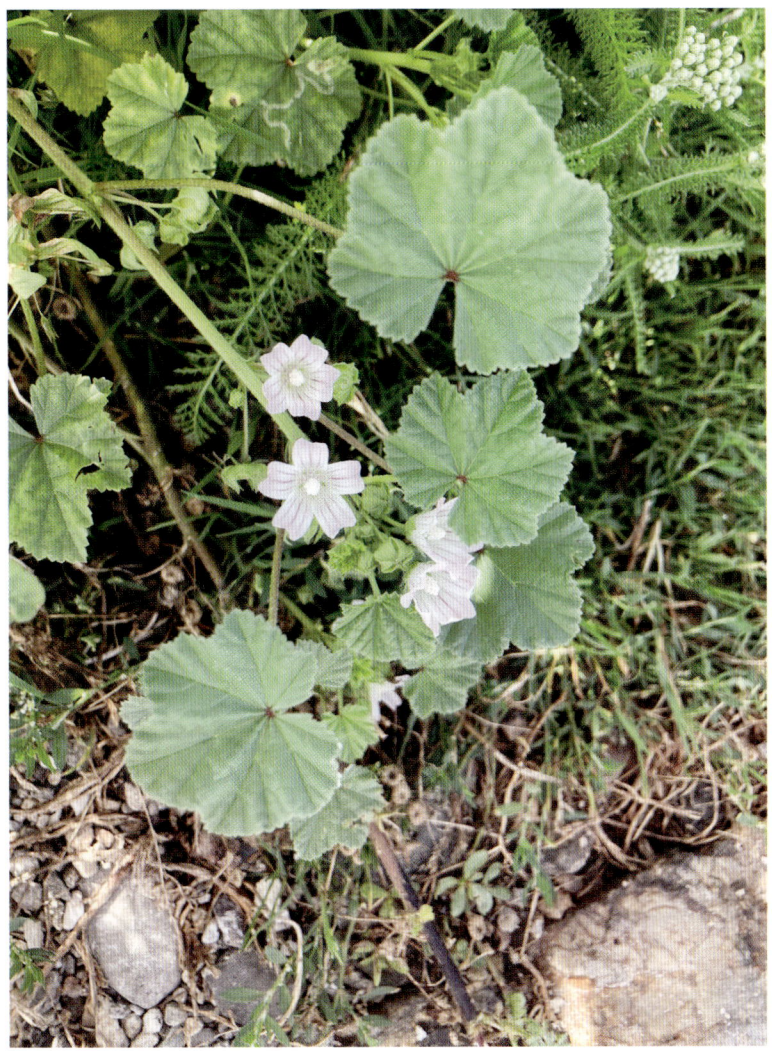

Mallow along the path, Appledore Island, ME

CHAPTER VI

HIBERNATE

Mother Nature taught me to value rest. In the indigenous creation stories from cultures around the world, she is the main character who advocates for the wellbeing of all living things using her creative power to keep everything in the universe in balance. Early on in my experience painting outdoors, I discovered that the exhausting pace required to keep up with sunlight and weather simply did not improve with sheer grit and furious paint-handling. To paint the environment's spectacular displays of color, I needed to respect the wishes of the entire system controlled by Mother Earth and consider her overarching intuition.

Painting sessions improved significantly when I cut back on my plans and accepted hers. I trained and prepared to work within the limits of unseen forces displayed in simple planes of light before me. I picked up my pace to respond to the visual stimulation outdoors using a direct code of marks and colors. I selected my medium using a strategy that complemented the conditions. For example, I chose pastels to work in the most difficult locations with fast moving weather because the saturated sticks of pigment adapt without the added steps of mixing on a palette. When I had the luxury of a somewhat steadier condition and opted to use liquid paint, I organized my palette to make quick grabs for color, located each time in the same place.

On the roller coaster of any creative process, my work on location got better, then failed miserably, and without warning, I would win a glimpse into what I was able to achieve. The most helpful adjustment to my process for painting on-site was taking a rest after every twenty-minute effort, walking away to clear my vision especially when things became gray. These short naps for my eyesight allowed me to clean my brushes and relax. Students, whose paintings regularly devolved into mud, also benefited from permission to stop and rest at twenty-minute intervals. I encouraged such check-ins to become routine because I could see what they had lost sight of; their choices no longer reflected the landscape's distinguished color range. Overtaking their vision was fatigue that made everything read the same. We all know examples of losing perspective, which stopping to take a break can restore. Sometimes we need to be reminded of the process that our body uses to stay in top form. Professionally, acknowledging that you require regular breaks takes courage and persistence.

My mother insisted on naps. These were grueling punishments when she needed it more than we did. Often referred to as "reading rests" because of the stack of books placed at the end of the bed, this was quiet time with the door closed. Her mother, my grandmother, was serious about napping, even at Disneyland. Though she lived in Los Angeles, she would get a room at the Disney Hotel just to nap during the long, overstimulating day of our visit. These were highly creative women, sensitive to their environment. Without question, we kids and our grandfather took their habits in stride.

Most parents know intuitively what research performed over thirty years ago has quantified in data for American business: productivity is improved significantly when employees, children, and adults are given rest. Unfortunately, our culture's notion of a highly successful individual is exemplified by someone who is frenetic and works continually, not a napper. But I have watched six-to-ten-foot-long sharks at the bottom of a sandy underwater riverbed being cleaned by remoras while relaxing under their care. Habits for rest and hibernation vary throughout the animal kingdom, with predators often paying the most attention.

Hidden in Plain Sight

Camouflage is a color strategy Mother Nature provides to creatures most vulnerable in the wild to prevent others from disturbing their siesta. It is no accident that clown fish, sporting Halloween regalia in orange, black, and white, prefer to cuddle-up within the enveloping orange pumpkin anemone. Color and shape that align with the background drop away distinctions for an effective disguise. Zebras all come dressed in the same striped suit, allowing the herd to look like one massive animal. Is it coming or going? The form-fitted, rhythmic pattern of grasses in light and shadow of the whole diminishes the contour of the individual. Their movement is hard to fix in your sight as they run together in a group.

Can you even imagine the "oversensitive" insult hurled at the magnificent octopus whose kaleidoscope of color concealment—magically performed by specialized pigmented organs on the cephalopods skin called *chromatophores*—activates when sensing danger and in need of cover? Naturally, introverted humans display their sensitivity to light and color in muted dress to blend in with the crowd in the fashion of cephalopods, while those who crave the spotlight make their presence an event, like a mating peacock exploiting the opposite light strategy of saturated, distinctive color. Both are Mother Nature's ideas, picked up on and borrowed to join the human race, where they will be seen, live comfortably, and thrive.

It is common for me to arrive at a home or office to be greeted at the door by the client wearing the colors that surround him or her. I have found that most people learn to make specific color selections dressing themselves and also answer with their wardrobe colors when asked, "What color would you like?" in various situations. Over their lives, they fine-tune their personal palette, feeling good about a curated collection of hue that expresses their personality and has become comfortable to their eyes. Colors that enliven skin tone, contrast with hair or eye color, or express a particular style can bring attention to your presence and telegraph who you are or want to be. These may be the colors you get complimented on when worn around family and friends.

TRY THIS AT HOME

Materials: *Nature of Color*, Color-aid paper or Prismacolor pastels, scissors, glue stick

Take a look in your clothes closet and determine if your palette causes you to disappear at home—you may have made the same color choices for your walls, furniture, or rugs. Notice the saturation of colors that you feel good sporting and enjoy being seen in. In your field guide, make a series of eight squares that will serve to record the colors that you find repeated throughout your clothing collection. If your palette is vibrant, cut squares of Color-aid paper to glue into your workbook. For more subtle hues, use Prismacolor pastels, distinctive for their more natural look, to adjust the colors and make samples to fill the eight squares of your palette.

TRY THIS ON THE TRAIL

Materials: *Nature of Color*, Prismacolor or Color-aid paper, glue stick

While on your next walk on the beach or hike in the woods, find a spot that would offer good shelter if you were prevented from getting back to your car and driving home. Imagine the patterns and colors that could make your figure indistinguishable from your resting place in this environment for the night. How might the dark change the colors that you would use? Make an example of camouflage that would be the perfect disguise, being mindful of the color palette that you may be wearing today and the wardrobe colors recorded in your field guide. Could you disappear into this habitat wearing your hiking attire?

Design Home as Habitat

The peaceful expression accompanying the stages of sleep on the face of a child, or animals great and small, signal the transformative power that rest provides and the requirement of giving over to the need for a restorative snooze. Had my father inadvertently shortened the life of our beloved pet desert tortoise who disappeared each year at about the same time? We had no idea when we followed Dad, armed with a long-handled shovel, into the canyon on a "Humphrey Hunt" that this old friend was trying to hibernate. Humphrey did not wish to be returned to our yard at that moment of well-deserved rest, to be sat upon and cajoled in our play as he circled the yard with the sun.

We do not hibernate, though medical science has shown that humans have the ability to do so. The change of seasons in many regions around the world is ushered in with distinctive color and light shifts accompanied by temperature changes affecting the way we feel and respond to our environment. Plants display the procession of color into dormancy just as they impressed us with their cheerful shoots in springtime and the unforgettable blooms of summer. Many people look forward to these natural signals heralding a new season with a new routine. Rain, snow, and the increase in overcast weather for some is time that they "hibernate" indoors and do tasks unthinkable on a sunny day. Men long for and build "man caves" for themselves and other males to commune in the very conditions of hibernation. Writers can use the slower pace of darker days to think deeply and accomplish their work.

Colors that are exemplary of a particular time of the year can be replicated indoors to welcome the change of season and get us in the mood for cozier or more festive times ahead. Decor is chosen to either harmonize or offset the season's cool or warm temperatures, the quality of the light, and the length of days. Those of us who long for eternal sun can use the effect of color mimicry to create the light conditions that we crave in rooms that serve more social or active functions for the family. For quiet study, contemplation, or sleep, the cool and dark palette of winter is at the ready to inspire.

Rest is my creative "supercharger" that never fails my practice as an architectural color designer. I have time built into my process to allow me to draw on the mysterious back-up system that I believe everyone has. In repose, the sights and sensations that I have taken in during the day mingle with my unconscious and my imagination gets to work. The marinating of ideas allows me to solve problems magically. Don't ask me how. Sometimes I wake in the early morning and realize that I have the perfect design. I will get up and write down what I do not want to lose track of by returning for more sleep.

I've depended upon my trusted back-up system throughout my life. "I'll sleep on it" is not a line that I use myself, but it is definitely the last word for a consultation that isn't going anywhere. I do not want to appear glib, but I need time to use my drive home or another mindless task when sleep or quiet is impossible. Just doing dishes or cleaning brushes frees my mind for the breakthrough solutions. Henri Matisse, known for pinning current paintings to his bedroom wall, was allowing himself the benefit of seeing his work indirectly from his peripheral vision. Now who is going to question that example of rest required in a creative process that works? Our stressful, overstimulating lives slow down and fall into a more manageable rhythm simply with a walk in nature or a half hour of gardening in the sunshine and fresh air. Once you have seen the effects of strategic rest, I'm sure you will add outdoor time to your work process, even as a relief strategy when you feel you are on the brink of a minor meltdown.

TRY THIS AT HOME

Materials: *Nature of Color*, Prismacolors or paint chip samples

Imagine the qualities of a space that creates a mood to put you to sleep. Take time to identify colors that encourage you to rest. Maybe you enjoy a warm blanket tucking you in regardless of the seasonal temperature; or maybe you are someone who is triggered to doze in a room with the warm glow of wood; or maybe you depend on a dark, cool, quiet space to tune out distractions. Colors of shade in the tropics, walls that dampen the light for a daytime nap or simply go dark with the sun's disappearance at the end of a day, may fit your notion of slumber.

This exercise will help you articulate what inspires *your* circadian rhythm, but will not necessarily meet the needs of other family members or your clients. If you are having trouble thinking of specific colors that work for your bedroom retreat, head over to a paint store and consider the temperature that would be optimum, then look for a color in the rack of paint chips that reflects both the physical and emotional thermostat setting you aim for in your room to repose. Identifying a restful palette of color that works for you will help you in turn respond to a client's request to create a truly personal oasis of calm or guide other family members to condition their bedrooms to fulfill the function so important to life and happiness.

Design Home as Habitat, Cont.

I succumbed to the persuasive power of Mother Nature's seasonal color palette when I tried to finish a museum mural of a salt marsh that I had started painting in the spring, but I was delayed due to an installation schedule slowdown that postponed the finish until fall. As I began the final phase to paint the incomplete areas, I caught myself selecting the colors of autumn I saw on walks to and from work. My internal color clock was fighting the image from an earlier time, very different in the quality of light and foliage. Despite my best effort to fake the earlier season, I decided that the Natural History Museum's salt marsh display would radiate more authentic color details if I reworked them altogether and drew from the current season's landscape of color. This process taught me to avoid correcting a painting from a different time of year when authentic natural color is desired.

Graphic and media designers, interior designers, and architects all know the value of incorporating visually inactive spaces of rest in their designs. These creatives learn in art school that a viewer has only so much bandwidth to focus attention and follow your intent. Quiet space allows the public to move through a layout at a comfortable pace, visually inspecting and navigating. Users of public architecture write reviews with comments like, "It follows a natural flow" or "There's a peacefulness," and say that they "know where they are going" when the design feeds their visual-locating curiosity at a comfortable pace.

Color is a vehicle to move the user from place to place and can even adjust the three-dimensional proportions at the end of the building process with color illusion simply to enhance the experience of habitat or to correct design flaws. I am most often called to join a new project when there is a big, expensive problem. The developer or builder wants the blunder to go away. What might have been picked up on elevations or the model with more careful consideration now stands shouting in three-dimension. With tools such as camouflage and color perspective, I have helped scale down over-sized doorways, moved a wall back into place without demolition and reconstruction, and opened windows to the million-dollar view. For solving these and many other issues, I relied on a visual sleight-of-hand borrowed from nature.

Color is the most underutilized power-tool in the creation of the built environment. In a sustainable model of the building trade, color beats all other methods for providing the biggest bang for the buck. Hue transforms our visual perceptions to meet our physiological requirements for habitation and life here on earth. Why not take advantage of Mother Nature's generosity first before engineering and manufacturing solutions that can create unforeseen problems for the ecosystem that gives us life?

My father's often repeated definition of "genius" was "the simplest solution for a complex problem." I took these words to heart and was on the lookout for ways to make color choices that reflected the elegance of good design in concert with respect for the natural world. Dad's engineering career during the 1960s and '70s space race of invention influenced him to deduce that "geniuses are inherently lazy"—always looking for a solution that takes the work out of the problem. As a mother and naturalist, I look back with hindsight to question my father's conclusion. I imagine that the geniuses he admired practiced in a highly stimulating, pressurized environment and needed to get more rest, but in lacking it, valued quick and simple solutions. They used the latest and greatest manufactured and natural resources that then seemed unlimited, and they did so without much regard for environmental impact. Now, our natural world is visibly trashed with material "solutions" that do not coexist with the balance of nature and are not "genius" in my nature-centric view.

Many great minds today are tackling how to stop the cycle of waste and voracious consumption, but global manufacturing still is slow to embrace the eco-minded alternatives. This is why I propose a greater role for color and illusion in solving the planet's problems. One example might be how the public may choose to rehabilitate its city centers rather than spreading out into nearby landscapes. The use of color and illusion can greatly change how citizens experience their public spaces. For example, in the recently built Q-line of New York City's subway, illusion was created in many of the new stations by taking wall-tile color to the next level, showing not only tiled versions of famous artists' work, but also for guiding foot traffic flow, using reflective ceilings to reduce the feeling of being underground, and generally making the riders feel safer and less stressed.

Color decisions are a part of every discipline where sight is a factor. Daily, humans around the globe see the results of their color selections at home or in the workplace with either satisfaction or frustration. When asked, "What color would you like?" many depend on old reliables. Your favorite bike color becomes the hue that you choose for your first car, when a color more suited to the heat of LA might be a better idea. That white car, so cool for the Hollywood set, is not so much suited for New England's environmental conditions, like mud season. Consider a roof that needs to be replaced and requires a color for the shingles. Your choice can shed the hot sun or absorb it, assisting the cooling system or making the third-floor office unbearable in the summer. Personal selections come with longstanding consequences when materials are costly and limited.

Neutral colors are considered a safe choice by many homeowners. But what does "neutral" really mean? If you think about it, a color can cause an object to merge with its surroundings and be "neutralized" using basic camouflage's principles employed by all living things. Beiges and soft tans are the home-goods manufacturers' Neutral Palette, marketed to the housekeeper as good colors for hiding the offensive color of dirt. Gray is a newer addition to that list, a "forgiving" color when wear and worry are involved. Modern, industrial design has focused our color-way attention on gray to align with metals and man-made materials of its edgy, repurposed look. The visually illusive quality that gray brings to a design sits back in a supporting role.

Materials: *Nature of Color*, Prismacolor pastels or Color-aid paper

Make a list of your "go-to" colors for your home's interior. What are your influences—colors you might use for cover, to create desired light conditions, or to complement choices that you are committed to as part of the family palette that supports heritage, heirlooms, collections, hand-me-downs, and art?

This exercise follows the same process as the personal color palette of examining your wardrobe. Identify eight squares of colors used repeatedly in your living spaces. Acknowledge the palette that influences you as it forms the atmosphere of your habitat. What adjustments might you want to make to fine-tune your interior space to fit your view of nature outdoors? What color would work with existing family color history? Which of the new insights foraged from your treks outside will help you rework the space, to claim it as your own? Can you imagine an interior where primary red is a neutral?

Color Wisdom

Artists throughout history have created work on location, revealing their regard for Mother Nature's wisdom. Early cave painters in France (maybe the first Artists-in-Residence) cleverly made use of the rock wall's bas relief with natural pigments to represent animals desired for food. Paul Cézanne could see that his paintings expressed nature's intangibles when he left it to the viewer to actively participate in reassembling the unfinished color patches of

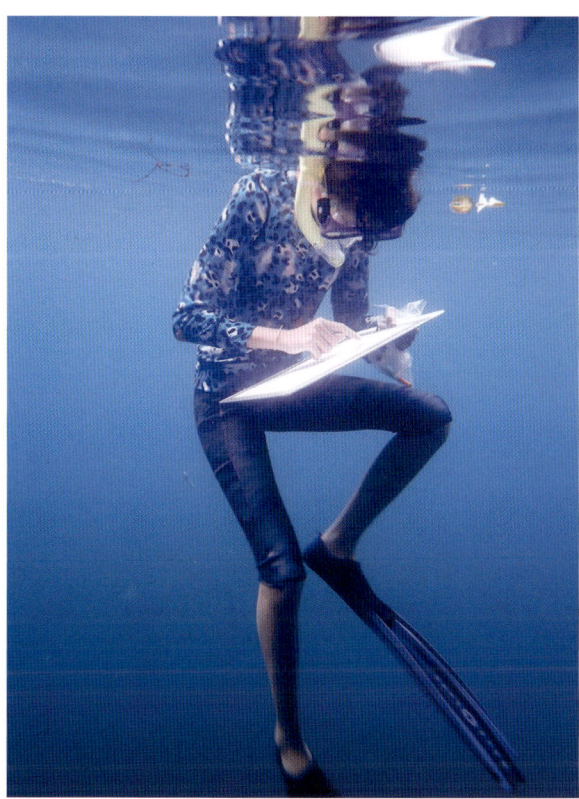

El hard at work, Dr. Carsten Grupstra

Mont Sainte-Victoire. American painters of the Hudson River School produced rapturous portraits of America as a promised land, putting Mother Earth on a pedestal. Luminists like Martin Johnson Heade and Fitz Henry Lane would go a step further and paint Mother Nature as the light and spirit they witnessed illuminating the coastal landscapes of their home.

Whether nature has long made an impression on your life, filled your dreams, and directed your desires, or you are discovering a new passion for the great outdoors, I encourage you to keep making note of your perceptions while marveling at the color in the landscape; the inexplicable relevance to whatever you do will appear with time. Discovering color someplace new now has a method. Making plans for staying connected to your source of wonderment has a process. You are an integral part of the magnificent systems you see outdoors, especially when you find your own innovative ways of seeing and creating. The responsibility for doing so is in respect for the delicate balance that Mother Nature bestows on each of us.

I have been conflicted about writing this book, fighting the fashioning of a step-by-step curriculum that could be seen as a color "How To." I have written about color using life lessons presented to me as precious gifts through a career as an artist, as one fascinated by nature, and curiously seeking guidance to share with my family, friends, students, and clients. The tools for shaping your habitat, expressing the color of a weather event, or using the physical power of the energy of the sun are shared here to guide your path, not direct it. Rather, I aim to get you going on more adventures outdoors where you can't help but see and study nature. Take the trail where it leads you.

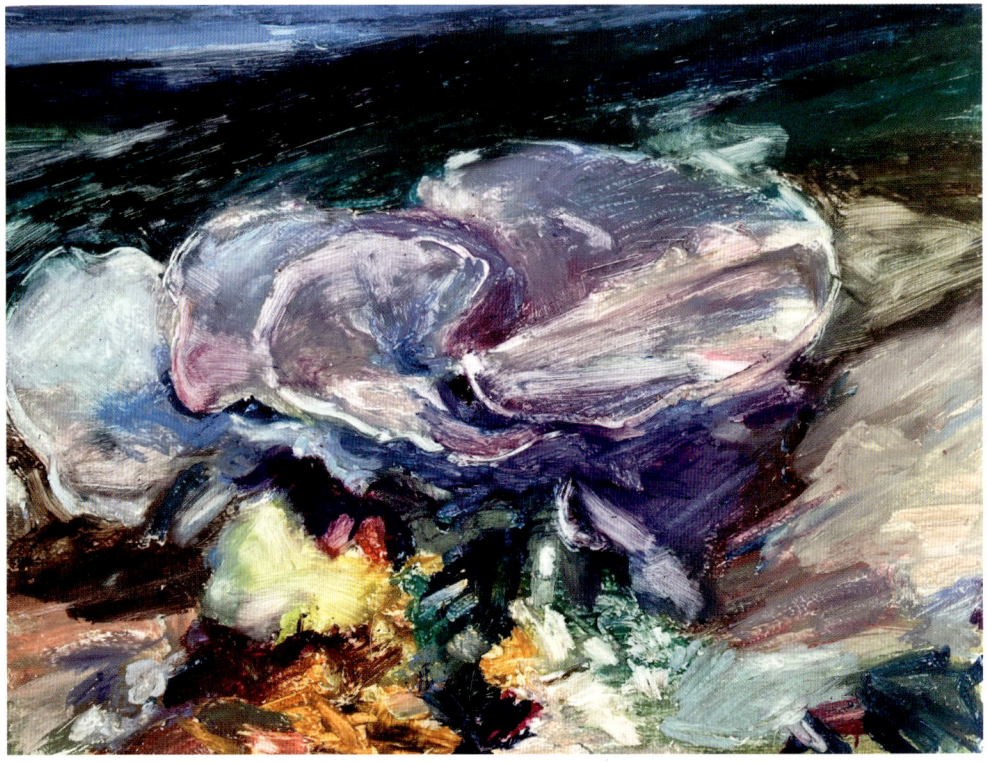

"Plate Coral, Inner Toach," oil stick on YUPO paper, Palau

A student in a color class a few years ago repeatedly asked me to tell her my favorite white when we were alone before class. She was willing to "trade" a white that a well-known area builder told her he used in all of his homes. I explained that I didn't have color favorites, that hue works for a particular lighting situation and context in the way that perennial plants are wonderful when they fit the conditions; this illustrates the gardener's adage, "Weeds are flowers in the wrong place." I repeated that the concepts that we were discussing in class and trying out in exercises would help her make color choices for architecture under any circumstance and that she would find the theory more usable as she practiced. That didn't satisfy her. At the end in her class review, she complained that I had kept all my "secrets" about color to myself.

There is no secret sauce or recipe for using color in three-dimensional space in a way that works exactly how you might think. No one single right formula or color system, trending or not. The site conditions and visible context make your choices more obvious on location, and these need to be understood for the unique expectations of the user.

You needn't follow my approach after giving it a go to start your own journey outdoors to use the color medium. My experience teaching tells me that the students who I disappoint the most are struggling with the concepts and will run into a situation long after I am out of their orbit that causes my voice to cycle into their consciousness again when they are ready to learn. It is natural to question and to stick with what works for you until you find that it doesn't. Sometimes color consternations take a few months, other times a few years. One student came to class in a rush and announced that he had tried the previous week's exercise again over the weekend and "would never see blue and orange the same way again." I was thrilled for him. I often wonder about these exclamations. I know that I am only one nudge on these students' color paths.

The more you tap color resources, the more intriguing they become when they are illusive, conditional, or even overwhelming in their complexity. I hope *Nature of Color* will continue to help you engage with color on many levels—personal, scientific, and artistic. Searching for color and how it shapes our view is a lifelong sport in which there is always something new to learn. Whether you are a seasoned pro or a newcomer to the game, respect your color wisdom. Follow your first color impressions and bravely take a chance on hitting your mark.

I write this last chapter as the season is shifting in light and color through autumn towards winter here in New England. The air temperature drops at night and seldom rises above 70 degrees during the day. I try to get the last few swims in the quarry where I am painting. I asked my son if the fish were really changing color as they appeared to be doing along with the milfoil weed. "Of course," was his answer, as he elaborated that the blue gill's camouflage might be more subtle than a flounder's adjustments to the ocean floor. He shared another bit of science that I had also forgotten to take into consideration when I described the icy cold dive entry through the leaves that now littered the water's surface. "Water temperatures can change by the hour throughout the day due to mixing."

Indeed, my swim buddy and I discovered the west-facing wall was a heater for the surface water in the afternoon sun where we lingered to admire the color and warm up before the swim back. Warm orange granite with shimmering green and yellow birch leaves rustled in the wind, the fish have grown and now had a red cast, and the milfoil was almost indistinct from the ochre rock of the submerged steps left behind by the quarrymen. The afternoon plunge gathered color insights to last a few days until another window appears to take another final look.

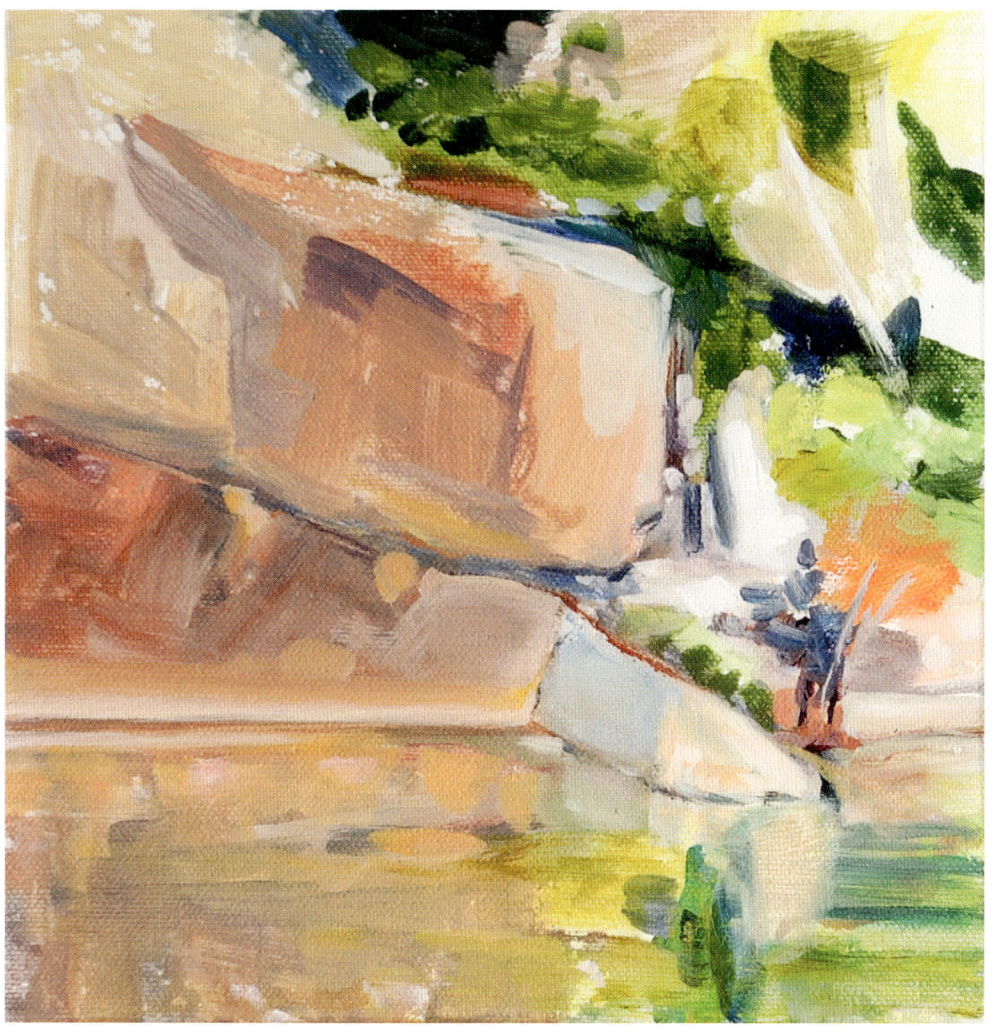

"Summer Quarry Wall," acrylic on canvas, Lanesville, MA

GLOSSARY OF TERMS

A

aerial perspective The original term for the optical effects of color in space prior to the advent of the airplane; current terms: *color perspective, spatial color.*

afterimage An image that remains visible, though fleetingly, to the viewer once the object has been removed.

air bladder An air-filled sac found in certain animals and plants, especially marine and aquatic species.

aquatic Relating to water.

artist's method The practices associated with creating art.

B

bas relief A sculptural relief in which forms extend only slightly from the background.

C

camouflage The ability to blend in with the surroundings and become invisible.

cephalopod Member of the molluscan class of marine animals such as squid, octopus, cuttlefish, or nautilus.

chromatic value Lightness or darkness of a hue.

chromatophores A pigment-bearing cell in an animal capable of camouflage.

chromoluminarism The separation of areas of hue into individual dots that interact optically.

color blind Unable to distinguish certain colors or, in some cases, all hues.

Color Field Painting An art movement originating in New York City during the 1940s and 1950s, characterized by large canvases stained and expressively painted using large fields of color for optical effects.

color orienteering Looking for and locating color in nature.

color patches Dabs or brush marks of paint.

color perspective The modern term for the optical reality of color changing with distance.

color receptors Cone-shaped cells in the human retina that detect different wavelengths of light in regulating color vision. See also *cones, rods.*

color value The lightness or darkness of a color.

color wheel A circular construct representing a rainbow of color used to explore the relationship of hues in the visible spectrum.

Color-aid paper The brand name for swatch books of silkscreened paper used by students and professionals to experiment with relationships of hue in two dimensions.

colortropism The orientation of an organism to color as with other external stimuli.

complementary colors A color and its opposite: red and green; blue and orange; yellow and purple. See also *opposite color*.

cones The photoreceptors responsible for color vision. See also *rods* and *color receptors*.

D

deep lookers Aspirational, close visual inspectors.

detritus Waste.

double entendre A word or a phase open to two interpretations, one of which may be risqué.

F

Found Color Color found while exploring outdoors, photographed, and savored; a color experience that causes wonder and awe (a study practice similar to making use of the Found Object).

frontal system A weather system that is created when two masses of air of different temperature, humidity, and density collide, establishing a boundary between them and a variety of weather conditions.

G

ground The surface used by a visual artist, an illusion to earth's surface and gravity.

H

hue Another word for color.

I

in situ On-site.

internal light meter A developed skill for sensing the intuitive.

intertidal zone The area between high and low tide along the coastal region of the marine habitat.

L

landscape A principal subject of Western art.

layout A visual order or design for artwork.

Light Reflective Value (LRV) A calibration of the light reflected off the surface of an object; also *Light Reflectance Value*.

linear perspective drawing Representation of the visible world in three-dimensional space on a two-dimensional surface.

local color A term to describe color that is next to the viewer.

M

mackerel sky A cloud formation of waves of cirrocumulus or altocumulus clouds that resembles a pattern of fish scales.

mare's tails A type of cirrus cloud that forms at high elevations in the atmosphere from strong winds, creating the horsetail shape, signaling a change in the weather.

marine. Of or pertaining to the sea or matters connected with the sea.

medium A material used to create visual art.

metaphor A figure of speech or visual art form in which an object or idea is used in place of another to suggest a likeness.

mind's eye The ability to imagine something vividly.

N

neuropathways A complex network of neurons in the brain that enable the transmission of signals from one part of the brain to another.

neuroscience A scientific field that studies the structure, function, development, and disorders of the nervous system.

O

opposite color The color that is derived by mixing two primary colors. See also *complementary colors*.

optic Relating to the eye and vision.

orienteering A navigating challenge.

P

plein-air, also *en-plein-air*. A French term for painting outdoors, on location.

paint chips Industry-grade samples of available color from the company's product line.

palette A selection of colors used together; a flat surface to hold paint for mixing and applying.

pastel Color that has been diluted with white.

pastels A color-drawing medium made from pure pigment mixed with a binder to form a stick.

perception Knowledge of the world gained through the five senses.

phototropism The orientation of a plant or other organism in a response to light; also *phototropic*.

picture frame The dimensional form of a picture plane.

picture plane The physical surface of the drawing or painting.

pixelation A digital image processing technique that reduces the resolution of an image to dots of color.

plumb A weighted line that reveals the vertical alignment of something.

Pointillism The term given to the work of Georges Seurat, Paul Signac, and their followers, inspired by optical theory explored in the nineteenth century, who painted using small dabs of color to create a stimulating effect of natural light.

primary color Red, blue, and yellow; considered to be the primary colors to mix all other colors.

projected image An afterimage that appears as a reflex response to fatigue caused by focused visual attention.

pure color One that has the greatest saturation of hue and is not mixed with another.

R

retina The light-sensitive membrane covering the back wall of the eyeball.

rods Photoreceptor cells in the outer region of the retina that improve sight in low light and provide peripheral vision. See also *cones, color receptors.*

S

sand painting Pouring colored sand or sand mixed with dry pigments on a surface to create a design used by Navajo and Pueblo tribes for celebrations and ceremonies; also known as dry painting.

saturated Highly pigmented.

secondary color Three colors that can be made by mixing only two of the three primary colors together: orange, green, and purple.

sensation A physical feeling or perception resulting from something that happens to or comes into contact with the body.

somatic Of the body.

spatial color See *color perspective*.

square A figure with four equal straight sides and four right angles.

Studio Chiaroscuro A technique that uses strong contrasts between light and dark to create a sense of volume and mass.

sunsation A physical feeling or perception resulting from the sun.

synapse Junction between two neurons (axon to dendrite) or between a neuron and a muscle.

synesthesia A neurological phenomenon in which stimulation of one sense involuntarily triggers experiences in another sense.

T

temperature inversion A layer in the atmosphere where the air temperature increases with height (in contrast to the normal situation in which air is warmer near the ground and colder at higher altitudes).

tetrachromatic vision A genetic mutation giving over 10 percent of women a fourth photoreceptor that allows them to see exponentially more colors than most people with three cones.

trichromatic vision Photoreceptors that discern three colors of light.

V

viewfinder A simple paper aid for drawing or painting; used to define that which is within the picture frame, as with a camera viewfinder.

visceral Obtained through intuition rather than from observation or reason.

Sources for Definitions:

Learn That Foundation. learnthat.org

Merriam-Webster Dictionary

Kimberly Collins Jermain

The Tate Museum. tate.org.uk/ar/art-terms

BIBLIOGRAPHY

Agoston, G.A. *Color Theory and Its Application in Art and Design*. Springer-Verlag, 1920.

Albers, Josef. *Interaction of Color*. Yale University Press, 1963.

Alter, Adam. *Drunk Tank Pink: And Other Unexpected Forces That Shape How We Think, Feel and Behave*. Penguin Press, 2013.

Appleton, Jay. *The Experience of Landscape*. John Wiley & Sons, 1975; California Press, 1969.

Birren, Faber. *Creative Color*. Reinhold Publishing Corporation, 1961.

Birren, Faber. *Color, Form and Space*. Reinhold Publishing Corporation, 1961.

Carlson, John F., NA. *Carlson's Guide to Landscape Painting*. Sterling Publishing Company, Inc., 1953.

Gage, John. *Color and Culture: Practice and Meaning from Antiquity to Abstraction*. California University Press, 1993.

Gage, John. *Color and Meaning: Art, Science and Symbolism*. University of California Press, 1999.

Gregory, R.L. *Eye and Brain: The Psychology of Seeing*. McGraw-Hill Book Company, 1966.

Grimely, Chris and Mimi Love. *Color Space and Style: All the Details Interior Designers Need to Know but Can Never Find*. Rockport Publishers, Inc., 2007.

Hoffman, Donald D. *Visual Intelligence* W.W. Norton & Company, Inc., 1998.

Iva. "The Impact of Sleep on Creativity." https://www.countingsheep.net/sleep-and-creativity. October 3, 2019.

Kellert, Stephen R. *Birthright: People and Nature in the Modern World*. Yale University Press, 2012.

Kemp, Martin. *Visualizations: The Nature Book of Art and Science*. University of California Press, 2000.

Lamb, Tevor and Janine Bourriau. *Colour: Art and Science*. Darwin College, 1995.

Lehrer, Jonah. *Imagine: How Creativity Works*. Houghton Mifflin, Harcourt, 2012.

Lehrer, Jonah. *Proust was a Neuroscientist*. Houghton Mifflin Company, 2007.

Libby, William Charles. *Color and the Structural Sense*. Prentice-Hall, Inc., 1974.

Machotka, Pavel. *Cézanne: Landscape into Art*. Yale University Press, 1996.

May, Matthew E. *In Pursuit of Elegance: Why the Best Ideas Have Something Missing*. Broadway Books, Random House, 2009.

Mehl, Richard. *Playing with Color*. Rockport Publishers, 2013.

Opara, Eddie and John Cantwell. *The Best Practices for Graphic Designers, Color Works* . Rockport Publishing, 2014.

Pauly, Daniéle (in association with Jérome Habersetzer). *Barragán: Space and Shadow, Walls and Color*. Birkauser–Basel, 2002.

Peralta, Sharon. "Tetrachromacy: Superhuman Vision?" All About Vision, May 1, 2023. https://www.allaboutvision.com/eye-care/eye-anatomy/tetrachromacy/.

Solso, Robert L. *Cognition and the Visual Arts*. Bradford Book Service, MIT Press, 1994.

Sussman, Ann and Justin B. Hollander. *Cognitive Architecture: Designing for How We Respond to the Built Environment*. Rutledge, 2015.

Swirnoff, Lois. *Dimensional Color*. Birkhauser Boston, Inc., 1989; W. W. Norton, New York, London, 2003.

Ware, Colin. *Visual Thinking for Design*. Morgan Kaufmann, 2008.

Watson, Ernest W. *Color and Method in Painting: As seen in the works of 12 American Painters*. Watson-Guptill Publications, Inc., 1942.

Wilson, Edward O. *Biophilia*. Harvard University Press, 1984.

ACKNOWLEDGMENTS

I offer this simple color workbook to the reader/rover in gratitude. Your walk in nature has now converged with the trail that I am exploring. Thank you for coming along.

I am indebted to my family of curious and inventive individuals playing outdoors to the rhythm of experimentation. My memories fill me with gratefulness for the gift of sharing unstructured time with you, stimulating conversations at the family dinner table, and the support with each step and struggle along our individual paths.

Our family's silent Indigenous elder influenced my approach to art and design implicitly. The enigma of Granny's curious wisdom launched my lifelong search for the roots of our father's culture, the Mi'kmaq people of Atlantic Canada. In writing this book, I better understand where our heritage expresses itself in me and am grateful that I am living at a time when I can freely acknowledge, without fear, the nature-inspired insights that shape my design ideas and visual art. I am especially grateful to Nate for allowing me to share his youthful explorations and insights.

I am humbled by the kindness of those who seek color wisdom. My clients and students exercise their mind's-eye trying out color principles with courage and grace. Many have become colleagues and lifelong friends. My design business has been shaped and supported by hundreds of color enthusiasts who've generously shared their perceptions and color consternations with me along the way.

A heartfelt thank you to my family of friends adventuring with me into the woods, onto the beach, in the mountains, on the marsh, and in and on the water—you have enriched my daily life. During the writing of this book, a few offered their home pools for me to swim, editorial guidance, writing companionship, and publishing leads. Those who have trekked into the bookmaking environment before me were generous with their help and encouragement. I am especially grateful to my artist friends who kindly shared their creative vision to help illustrate this book with their beautiful photography and paintings.

Everyone should have a friend like Claire Leggett! How lucky am I that she took on the challenge to help me edit the first draft—deftly applying her literary skill and sensitive ear for the artist's voice? Claire is the rarest of her species, able to find joy in the ideas of others and support them wholeheartedly. I am in awe of her skill and her kindness.

I could not have imagined the number of grants for materials, equipment, funded opportunities to travel, and artist residences provided to support my quest to explore and share an artful approach to science. Each experience has expanded my geographical range, while also informing my thoughts about color's importance to making our lives compatible with the habitat where we live on earth. Thank you:

Shoals Marine Lab, Appledore Island, ME

Dr. Kirstin Meyer-Kaiser and her team, Woods Hole Oceanographic Institution, Woods Hole, MA

Palau International Coral Reef Center

Manship Artists Residency

Once Upon Water, Arts Unfold, Pico Island, Azores

AquaLung

Puffin Foundation Ltd.

Turkey Land Cove Residency, Martha's Vineyard, MA

Hafnarfjörður Art Museum, Hafnarfjörður, Iceland

Armin E. Elsaesser, II Fellowship, Sea Education Association, Woods Hole, MA

Cat'Art International Arts Centre Residency, Ste. Colombe, France

Thank you to Familius—its publisher and gifted editorial team—for taking the leap of faith that my nature-centered workbook might illuminate the reader's latent color imagination. As our world faces existential environmental challenges, color provides a powerful tool for the support of a sustainable life. I am hopeful that this thoughtfully crafted publication will inspire readers and their families to employ their own heritage of life-skills in a creative practice using color to celebrate the value of all living things under the sun.

ABOUT THE AUTHOR

Kimberly Collins Jermain is a painter, teacher, and architectural color designer whose work explores coastal environments, weather phenomena, and the application of color principles for health and wellbeing in architecture. Since 1989, Kimberly has collaborated with homeowners, architects, interior designers, developers, and commercial property owners on color design projects. Her paintings of the intertidal zone of the North Atlantic document the human experience of a changing ocean ecosystem. Kimberly's creative career has been to share what she has observed in nature and put it to use for living well.

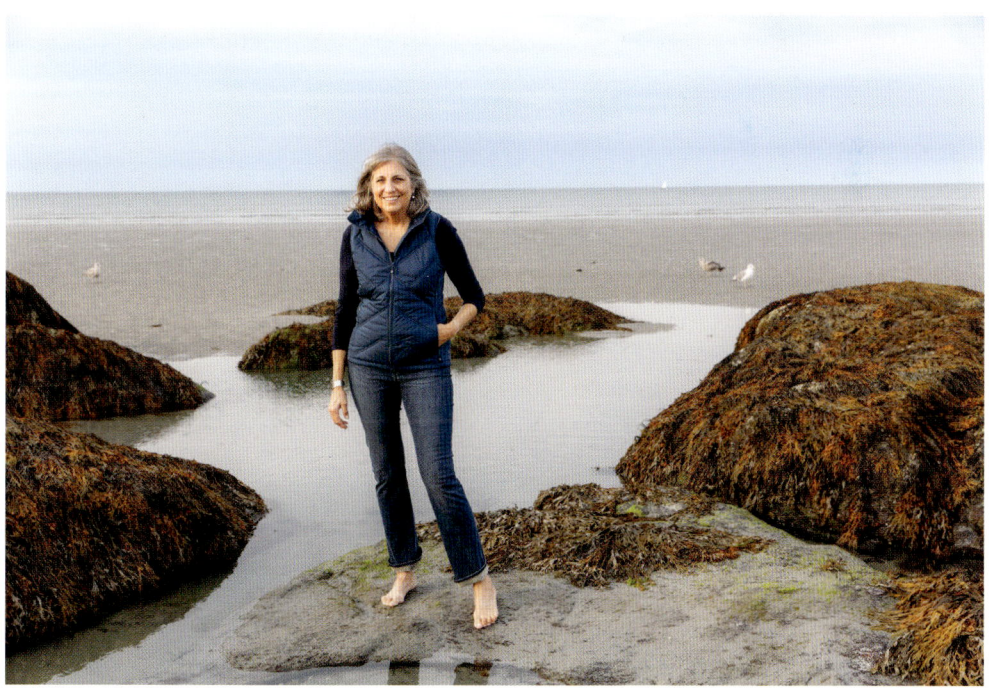

Kathy Tarantola Photography

ABOUT FAMILIUS

Visit Our Website: www.familius.com

Familius is a global trade publishing company that publishes books and other content to help families be happy. We believe that happy families are key to a better society and the foundation of a happy life. The greatest work anyone will ever do will be within the walls of his or her own home. And we don't mean vacuuming! We recognize that every family looks different and passionately believe in helping all families find greater joy, whatever their situation. To that end, we publish beautiful books that help families live our 10 Habits of Happy Family Life: *love together, play together, learn together, work together, talk together, heal together, read together, eat together, give together,* and *laugh together.* Further, Familius does not discriminate on the basis of race, color, religion, gender, age, nationality, disability, caste, or sexual orientation in any of its activities or operations. Founded in 2012, Familius is located in Sanger, California.

Connect

Facebook: www.facebook.com/familiusbooks

Pinterest: www.pinterest.com/familiusbooks

Instagram: @FamiliusBooks

TikTok: @FamiliusBooks

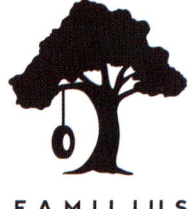

FAMILIUS

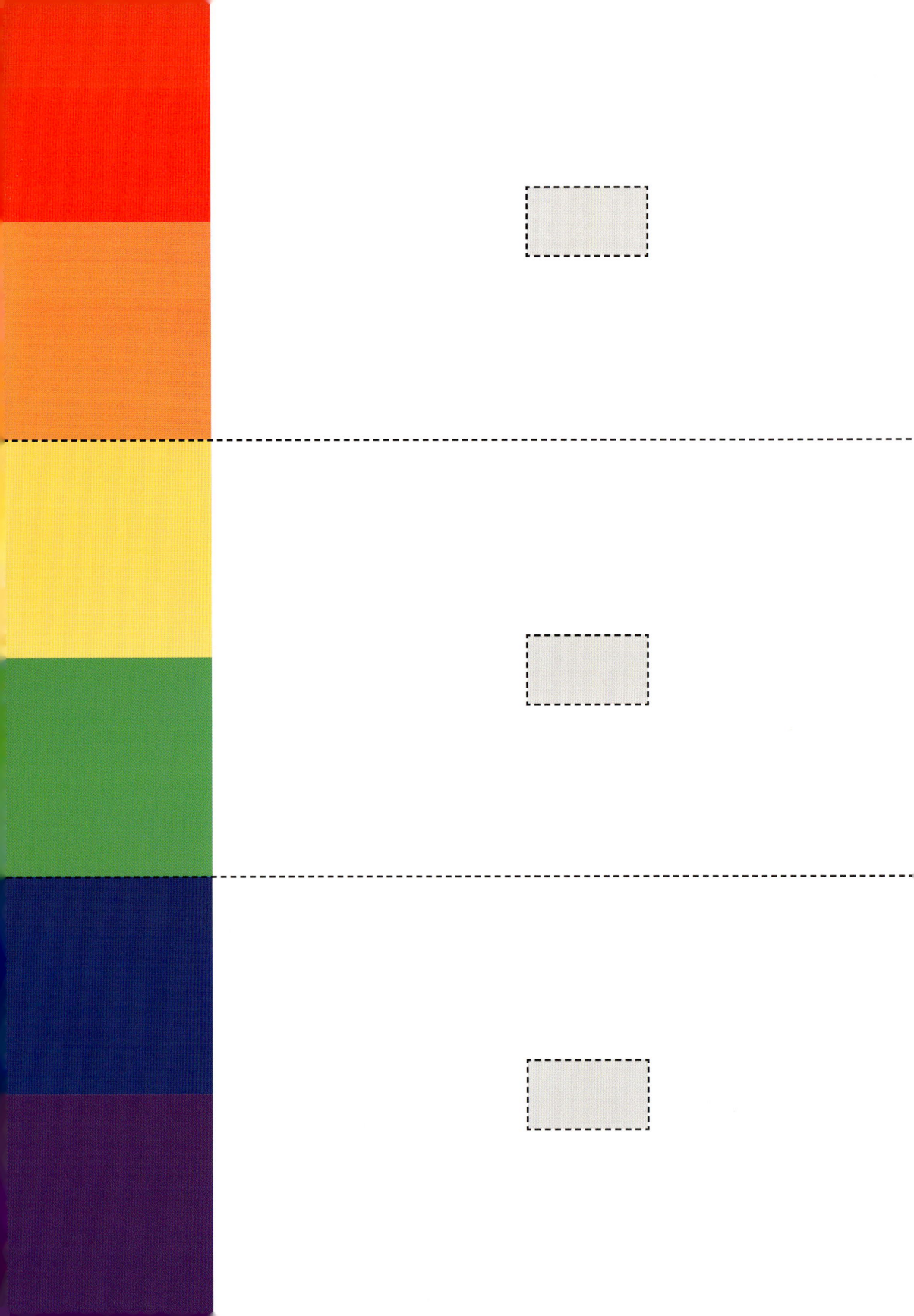

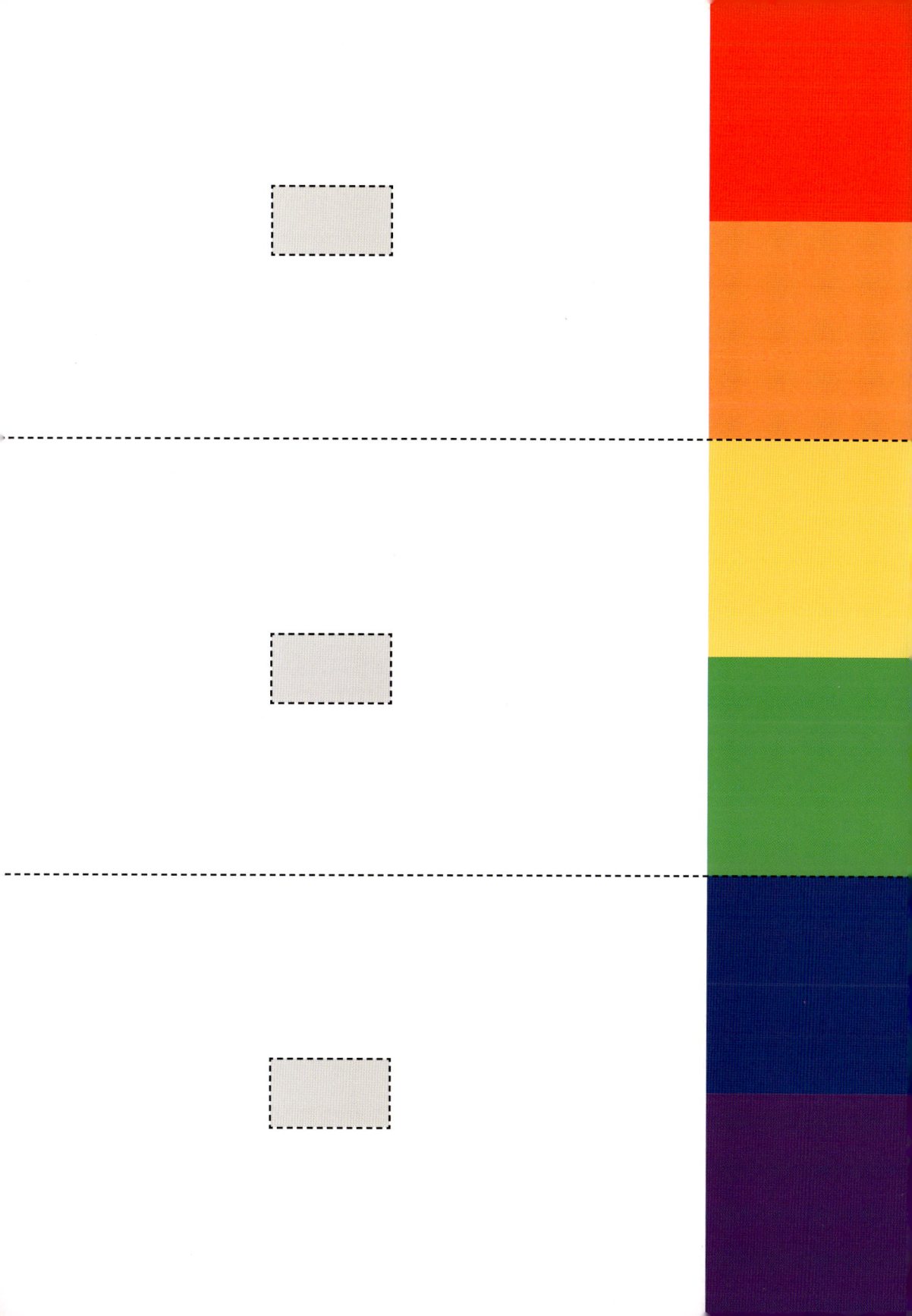